PENGUIN BOOKS — GREAT IDEAS

Anarchist Communism

Peter Kropotkin
1842–1921

Peter Kropotkin

Anarchist Communism

PENGUIN BOOKS — GREAT IDEAS

PENGUIN BOOKS

UK | USA | Canada | Ireland | Australia
India | New Zealand | South Africa

Penguin Books is part of the Penguin Random House group
of companies whose addresses can be found at
global.penguinrandomhouse.com.

Penguin
Random House
UK

First published in book form in French as *La Conquête du Pain* 1892
First published in English as *The Conquest of Bread* 1906
Revised edition published 1913
This extract, using the 1913 text, first published in Penguin Classics 2020

004

Set in 12/15 pt Dante MT Std
Typeset by Jouve (UK), Milton Keynes
Printed and bound in Great Britain by Clays Ltd, Elcograf S.p.A.

A CIP catalogue record for this book
is available from the British Library

ISBN: 978-0-241-47240-8

Contents

1 *Our Riches*

The human race has travelled a long way, since those remote ages when men fashioned their rude implements of flint and lived on the precarious spoils of hunting, leaving to their children for their only heritage a shelter beneath the rocks, some poor utensils – and Nature, vast, unknown and terrific, with whom they had to fight for their wretched existence.

During the long succession of agitated ages which have elapsed since, mankind has nevertheless amassed untold treasures. It has cleared the land, dried the marshes, hewn down forests, made roads, pierced mountains; it has been building, inventing, observing, reasoning; it has created a complex machinery, wrested her secrets from Nature, and finally it pressed steam and electricity into its service. And the result is, that now the child of the civilized man finds at its birth, ready for its use, an immense capital accumulated by those who have gone before him. And this capital enables man to acquire, merely by his own labour combined with the labour of others, riches surpassing the dreams of the fairy tales of the Thousand and One Nights.

The soil is cleared to a great extent, fit for the reception of the best seeds, ready to give a rich return for the skill and labour spent upon it – a return more than sufficient for all the wants of humanity. The methods of rational cultivation are known.

On the wide prairies of America each hundred men, with the aid of powerful machinery, can produce in a few months enough wheat to maintain ten thousand people for a whole year. And where man wishes to double his produce, to treble it, to multiply it a hundredfold, he *makes* the soil, gives to each plant the requisite care, and thus obtains enormous returns. While the hunter of old had to scour fifty or sixty square miles to find food for his family, the civilized man supports his household, with far less pains, and far more certainty, on a thousandth part of that space. Climate is no longer an obstacle. When the sun fails, man replaces it by artificial heat; and we see the coming of a time when artificial light also will be used to stimulate vegetation. Meanwhile, by the use of glass and hot-water pipes, man renders a given space ten and fifty times more productive than it was in its natural state.

The prodigies accomplished in industry are still more striking. With the co-operation of those intelligent beings, modern machines – themselves the fruit of three or four generations of inventors, mostly unknown – a hundred men manufacture now the stuff to provide ten thousand persons with clothing for two years. In well-managed coal-mines the labour of a hundred miners furnishes each year enough fuel to warm ten thousand families under an inclement sky. And we have lately witnessed the spectacle of wonderful cities springing up in a few months for international exhibitions, without interrupting in the slightest degree the regular work of the nations.

And if in manufactures as in agriculture, and as indeed through our whole social system, the labour, the discoveries and the inventions of our ancestors profit chiefly the few, it is none the less certain that mankind in general, aided by the creatures of steel and iron which it already possesses, could already procure an existence of wealth and ease for every one of its members.

Truly, we are rich – far richer than we think; rich in what we already possess, richer still in the possibilities of production of our actual mechanical outfit;

richest of all in what we might win from our soil, from our manufactures, from our science, from our technical knowledge, were they but applied to bringing about the well-being of all.

II

In our civilized societies we are rich. Why then are the many poor? Why this painful drudgery for the masses? Why, even to the best-paid workman, this uncertainty for the morrow, in the midst of all the wealth inherited from the past, and in spite of the powerful means of production, which could ensure comfort to all, in return for a few hours of daily toil?

The socialists have said it and repeated it unwearyingly. Daily they reiterate it, demonstrating it by arguments taken from all the sciences. It is because all that is necessary for production – the land, the mines, the highways, machinery, food, shelter, education, knowledge – all have been seized by the few in the course of that long story of robbery, enforced migration and wars, of ignorance and oppression, which has been the life of the human race before it had learned to subdue the forces of Nature. It is because, taking advantage of alleged rights acquired in the past, these few appropriate today two-thirds of the products of human labour, and then squander them in the most stupid and shameful way. It is because, having reduced the masses to a point at which they have not the means of subsistence for a month, or even for a week in advance, the few can allow the many to work, only on the condition of themselves receiving the lion's share. It is because these few prevent the remainder of men from producing the things they need, and force them to produce, not the necessaries of life for all, but whatever offers the greatest profits to the monopolists. In this is the substance of all socialism.

Take, indeed, a civilized country. The forests which once covered it have been cleared, the marshes drained, the climate improved. It has been made habitable. The soil, which bore formerly only a coarse vegetation, is covered today with rich harvests. The rock walls in the valleys are laid out in terraces and covered with vines. The wild plants, which yielded nought but acrid berries, or uneatable roots, have been transformed by generations of culture into succulent vegetables or trees covered with delicious fruits. Thousands of highways and railroads furrow the earth, and pierce the mountains. The shriek of the engine is heard in the wild gorges of the Alps, the Caucasus and the Himalayas. The rivers have been made navigable; the coasts, carefully surveyed, are easy of access; artificial harbours, laboriously dug out and protected against the fury of the sea, afford shelter to the ships. Deep shafts have been sunk in the rocks; labyrinths of underground galleries have been dug out where coal may be raised or minerals extracted. At the crossings of the highways great cities have sprung up, and within their borders all the treasures of industry, science and art have been accumulated.

Whole generations, that lived and died in misery, oppressed and ill-treated by their masters, and worn out by toil, have handed on this immense inheritance to our century.

For thousands of years millions of men have laboured to clear the forests, to drain the marshes, and to open up highways by land and water. Every rood of soil we cultivate in Europe has been watered by the sweat of several races of men. Every acre has its story of enforced labour, of intolerable toil, of the people's sufferings. Every mile of railway, every yard of tunnel, has received its share of human blood.

The shafts of the mine still bear on their rocky walls the marks made by the pick of the workman who toiled to excavate them. The space between each prop in the underground galleries might be marked as a miner's grave; and who can tell what each of these graves has cost, in tears, in privations, in unspeakable wretchedness to the family who depended on the scanty wage of the worker cut off in his prime by fire-damp, rockfall or flood?

The cities, bound together by railroads and waterways, are organisms which have lived through centuries. Dig beneath them and you find, one above another, the foundations of streets, of houses, of theatres, of public buildings. Search into their history and you will see how the civilization of the town, its industry, its special characteristics, have slowly grown and ripened through the co-operation of generations of its inhabitants before it could become what it is today. And even today, the value of each dwelling, factory and warehouse, which has been created by the accumulated labour of the millions of workers, now dead and buried, is only maintained by the very presence and labour of legions of the men who now inhabit that special corner of the globe. Each of the atoms composing what we call the Wealth of Nations owes its value to the fact that it is a part of the great whole. What would a London dockyard or a great Paris warehouse be if they were not situated in these great centres of international commerce? What would become of our mines, our factories, our workshops and our railways, without the immense quantities of merchandise transported every day by sea and land?

Millions of human beings have laboured to create

this civilization on which we pride ourselves today. Other millions, scattered through the globe, labour to maintain it. Without them nothing would be left in fifty years but ruins.

There is not even a thought, or an invention, which is not common property, born of the past and the present. Thousands of inventors, known and unknown, who have died in poverty, have co-operated in the invention of each of these machines which embody the genius of man.

Thousands of writers, of poets, of scholars, have laboured to increase knowledge, to dissipate error, and to create that atmosphere of scientific thought, without which the marvels of our century could never have appeared. And these thousands of philosophers, of poets, of scholars, of inventors, have themselves been supported by the labour of past centuries. They have been upheld and nourished through life, both physically and mentally, by legions of workers and craftsmen of all sorts. They have drawn their motive force from the environment.

The genius of a Séguin, a Mayer, a Grove, has certainly done more to launch industry in new directions than all the capitalists in the world. But men of genius are themselves the children of industry as well as of science. Not until thousands of steam-engines had been working for years before all eyes, constantly transforming heat into dynamic force, and this force into sound, light and electricity, could the insight of genius proclaim the mechanical origin and the unity of the physical forces. And if we, children of the nineteenth century, have at last grasped this idea, if we know now how to apply it, it is again because daily experience has prepared the way. The thinkers of the eighteenth century saw and declared it, but the idea remained undeveloped, because the eighteenth century had not grown up like ours, side by side with the steam-engine. Imagine the decades that might have passed while we remained in ignorance of this law, which has revolutionized modern industry, had Watt not found at Soho skilled workmen to embody his ideas in metal, bringing all the parts of his engine to perfection, so that steam, pent in a complete mechanism, and rendered more docile than a horse, more manageable than water, became at last the very soul of modern industry.

Every machine has had the same history – a long record of sleepless nights and of poverty, of disillusions and of joys, of partial improvements discovered by several generations of nameless workers, who have added to the original invention these little nothings, without which the most fertile idea would remain fruitless. More than that: every new invention is a synthesis, the resultant of innumerable inventions which have preceded it in the vast field of mechanics and industry.

Science and industry, knowledge and application, discovery and practical realization leading to new discoveries, cunning of brain and of hand, toil of mind and muscle – all work together. Each discovery, each advance, each increase in the sum of human riches, owes its being to the physical and mental travail of the past and the present.

By what right then can anyone whatever appropriate the least morsel of this immense whole and say – This is mine, not yours?

III

It has come about, however, in the course of the ages traversed by the human race, that all that enables man to produce and to increase his power of production has been seized by the few. Sometime, perhaps, we will relate how this came to pass. For the present let it suffice to state the fact and analyse its consequences.

Today the soil, which actually owes its value to the needs of an ever-increasing population, belongs to a minority who prevent the people from cultivating it – or do not allow them to cultivate it according to modern methods.

The mines, though they represent the labour of several generations, and derive their sole value from the requirements of the industry of a nation and the density of the population – the mines also belong to the few; and these few restrict the output of coal, or prevent it entirely, if they find more profitable investments for their capital. Machinery, too, has become the exclusive property of the few, and even when a machine incontestably represents the improvements added to the original rough invention by three or four generations of workers, it none the less belongs to a few owners. And if the descendants of the very inventor who constructed the first machine for lace-making, a century ago, were to present themselves today in a lace factory at Basle or Nottingham, and claim their rights, they would be told: 'Hands off! this machine is not yours', and they would be shot down if they attempted to take possession of it.

The railways, which would be useless as so much old iron without the teeming population of Europe, its industry, its commerce and its marts, belong to a few shareholders, ignorant perhaps of the whereabouts of the lines of rails which yield them revenues greater than those of medieval kings. And if the children of those who perished by thousands while excavating the railway cuttings and tunnels were to assemble one day, crowding in their rags and hunger, to demand bread from the shareholders, they would be met with bayonets and grapeshot, to disperse them and safeguard 'vested interests'.

In virtue of this monstrous system, the son of the worker, on entering life, finds no field which he may till, no machine which he may tend, no mine in which he may dig, without accepting to leave a great part of what he will produce to a master. He must sell his labour for a scant and uncertain wage. His father and his grandfather have toiled to drain this field, to build this mill, to perfect this machine. They gave to the work the full measure of their strength, and what more could they give? But their heir comes into the world poorer than the lowest savage. If he obtains leave to till the fields, it is on condition of surrendering a quarter of the produce to his master, and another quarter to the government and the middlemen. And this tax, levied upon him by the state, the capitalist, the lord of the manor and the middleman, is always increasing; it rarely leaves him the power to improve his system of culture. If he turns to industry, he is allowed to work – though not always even that – only on condition that he yield a half or two-thirds of the product to him whom the land recognizes as the owner of the machine.

We cry shame on the feudal baron who forbade

the peasant to turn a clod of earth unless he surrendered to his lord a fourth of his crop. We called those the barbarous times. But if the forms have changed, the relations have remained the same, and the worker is forced, under the name of free contract, to accept feudal obligations. For, turn where he will, he can find no better conditions. Everything has become private property, and he must accept, or die of hunger.

The result of this state of things is that all our production tends in a wrong direction. Enterprise takes no thought for the needs of the community. Its only aim is to increase the gains of the speculator. Hence the constant fluctuations of trade, the periodical industrial crises, each of which throws scores of thousands of workers on the streets.

The working people cannot purchase with their wages the wealth which they have produced, and industry seeks foreign markets among the monied classes of other nations. In the East, in Africa, everywhere, in Egypt, Tonkin or the Congo, the European is thus bound to promote the growth of serfdom. And so he does. But soon he finds that everywhere there are similar competitors. All the nations evolve on the same lines, and wars, perpetual wars, break out for the right of precedence in the market. Wars for the possession of the East, wars for the empire of the sea, wars to impose duties on imports and to dictate conditions to neighbouring states; wars against those 'blacks' who revolt! The roar of the cannon never ceases in the world, whole races are massacred, the states of Europe spend a third of their budgets in armaments; and we know how heavily these taxes fall on the workers.

Education still remains the privilege of a small minority, for it is idle to talk of education when the workman's child is forced, at the age of thirteen, to go down into the mine or to help his father on the farm. It is idle to talk of studying to the worker, who comes home in the evening wearied by excessive toil, and its brutalizing atmosphere. Society is thus bound to remain divided into two hostile camps, and in such conditions freedom is a vain word. The radical begins by demanding a greater extension of political rights, but he soon sees that the breath of liberty leads to the uplifting of the proletariat, and then he turns round, changes his opinions, and reverts to repressive legislation and government by the sword.

A vast array of courts, judges, executioners, policemen and gaolers is needed to uphold these privileges; and this array gives rise in its turn to a whole system of espionage, of false witness, of spies, of threats and corruption.

The system under which we live checks in its

turn the growth of the social sentiment. We all know that without uprightness, without self-respect, without sympathy and mutual aid, humankind must perish, as perish the few races of animals living by rapine, or the slave-keeping ants. But such ideas are not to the taste of the ruling classes, and they have elaborated a whole system of pseudo-science to teach the contrary.

Fine sermons have been preached on the text that those who have should share with those who have not, but he who would carry out this principle would be speedily informed that these beautiful sentiments are all very well in poetry, but not in practice. 'To lie is to degrade and besmirch oneself,' we say, and yet all civilized life becomes one huge lie. We accustom ourselves and our children to hypocrisy, to the practice of a double-faced morality. And since the brain is ill at ease among lies, we cheat ourselves with sophistry. Hypocrisy and sophistry become the second nature of the civilized man.

But a society cannot live thus; it must return to truth, or cease to exist.

Thus the consequences which spring from the original act of monopoly spread through the whole of social life. Under pain of death, human societies are forced to return to first principles: the means of production being the collective work of humanity, the product should be the collective property of the race. Individual appropriation is neither just nor service-able. All belongs to all. All things are for all men, since all men have need of them, since all men have worked in the measure of their strength to produce them, and since it is not possible to evaluate every-one's part in the production of the world's wealth.

All things for all. Here is an immense stock of tools and implements; here are all those iron slaves which we call machines, which saw and plane, spin and weave for us, unmaking and remaking, working up raw matter to produce the marvels of our time. But nobody has the right to seize a single one of these machines and say: 'This is mine; if you want to use it you must pay me a tax on each of your products', any more than the feudal lord of medieval times had the right to say to the peasant: 'This hill, this meadow belong to me, and you must pay me a tax on every sheaf of corn you reap, on every rick you build.'

All is for all! If the man and the woman bear their fair share of work, they have a right to their fair share of all that is produced by all, and that share is enough to secure them well-being. No more of such vague formulae as 'The right to work', or 'To each the whole result of his labour'. What we proclaim is *The Right to Well-Being: Well-Being for All!*

2 *Well-Being for All*

Well-being for all is not a dream. It is possible, realizable, owing to all that our ancestors have done to increase our powers of production.

We know, indeed, that the producers, although they constitute hardly one-third of the inhabitants of civilized countries, even now produce such quantities of goods that a certain degree of comfort could be brought to every hearth. We know further that if all those who squander today the fruits of others' toil were forced to employ their leisure in useful work, our wealth would increase in proportion to the number of producers, and more. Finally, we know that contrary to the theory enunciated by Malthus – that oracle of middle-class economics – the productive powers of the human race increase at a much more rapid ratio than its powers of reproduction. The more thickly men are crowded on the soil, the more rapid is the growth of their wealth-creating power.

Thus, although the population of England has only increased from 1844 to 1890 by 62 per cent, its production has grown, even at the lowest estimate, at double that rate – to wit, by 130 per cent. In France, where the population has grown more slowly, the increase in production is nevertheless very rapid. Notwithstanding the crises through which agriculture is frequently passing, notwithstanding state interference, the blood-tax (conscription), and speculative commerce and finance, the production of wheat in France has increased fourfold, and industrial production more than tenfold, in the course of the last eighty years. In the United States the progress is still more striking. In spite of immigration, or rather precisely because of the influx of surplus European labour, the United States have multiplied their wealth tenfold.

However, these figures give but a very faint idea of what our wealth might become under better conditions. For alongside of the rapid development of our wealth-producing powers we have an overwhelming increase in the ranks of the idlers and middlemen. Instead of capital gradually concentrating itself in a few hands, so that it would only be necessary for the community to dispossess a few millionaires and enter upon its lawful heritage – instead of this socialist forecast proving true, the exact reverse is coming to pass: the swarm of parasites is ever increasing.

In France there are not ten actual producers to every thirty inhabitants. The whole agricultural wealth of the country is the work of less than 7 million men, and in the two great industries, mining and the textile trades, you will find that the workers number less than 2½ million. But the exploiters of labour, how many are they? In the United Kingdom a little over 1 million workers – men, women and children – are employed in all the textile trades; less than 900,000 work the mines; much less than 2 million till the ground, and it appeared from the last industrial census that only a little over 4 million men, women and children were employed in all the industries.* So that the statisticians have to exaggerate all the figures in order to establish a maximum of 8 million producers to 45 million inhabitants. Strictly speaking, the creators of the goods exported from Britain to all the ends of the earth comprise only from 6 to 7 million workers. And what is the

---

* 4,013,711 now employed in all the 53 branches of different industries, including the State Ordnance Works, and 241,530 workers engaged in the construction and maintenance of railways, their aggregate production reaching the value of £1,041,037,000, and the net output being £406,799,000.

number of the shareholders and middlemen who levy the first fruits of labour from far and near, and heap up unearned gains by thrusting themselves between the producer and the consumer?

Nor is this all. The owners of capital constantly reduce the output by restraining production. We need not speak of the cartloads of oysters thrown into the sea to prevent a dainty, hitherto reserved for the rich, from becoming a food for the people. We need not speak of the thousand and one luxuries – stuffs, foods, etc., etc. – treated after the same fashion as the oysters. It is enough to remember the way in which the production of the most necessary things is limited. Legions of miners are ready and willing to dig out coal every day, and send it to those who are shivering with cold; but too often a third, or even one-half, of their number are forbidden to work more than three days a week, because, forsooth, the price of coal must be kept up! Thousands of weavers are forbidden to work the looms, although their wives and children go in rags, and although three-quarters of the population of Europe have no clothing worthy the name.

Hundreds of blast-furnaces, thousands of factories periodically stand idle, others only work half-time – and in every civilized nation there is a permanent population of about two million individuals who ask only for work, but to whom work is denied.

How gladly would these millions of men set to work to reclaim waste lands, or to transform ill-cultivated land into fertile fields, rich in harvests! A year of well-directed toil would suffice to multiply fivefold the produce of those millions of acres in this country which lie idle now as 'permanent pasture', or of those dry lands in the south of France which now yield only about eight bushels of wheat per acre. But men, who would be happy to become hardy pioneers in so many branches of wealth-producing activity, must remain idle because the owners of the soil, the mines and the factories prefer to invest their capital – taken in the first place from the community – in Turkish or Egyptian bonds, or in Patagonian gold-mines, and so make Egyptian fel-lahs, Italian emigrants and Chinese coolies their wage-slaves.

This is the direct and deliberate limitation of pro-duction; but there is also a limitation indirect and not of set purpose, which consists in spending human toil on objects absolutely useless, or destined only to satisfy the dull vanity of the rich.

It is impossible to reckon in figures the extent to which wealth is restricted indirectly, the extent to which energy is squandered, while it might have served to produce, and above all to prepare the machinery necessary to production. It is enough to cite the immense sums spent by Europe in armaments, for the sole purpose of acquiring control of the markets, and so forcing her own goods on neighbouring territories, and making exploitation easier at home; the millions paid every year to officials of all sorts, whose function it is to maintain the 'rights' of minorities – the right, that is, of a few rich men – to manipulate the economic activities of the nation; the millions spent on judges, prisons, policemen, and all the paraphernalia of so-called justice – spent to no purpose, because we know that every alleviation, however slight, of the wretchedness of our great cities is always followed by a considerable diminution of crime; lastly, the millions spent on propagating pernicious doctrines by means of the press, and news 'cooked' in the interest of this or that party, of this politician or of that group of speculators.

But over and above this we must take into account all the labour that goes to sheer waste – here, in keeping up the stables, the kennels and the retinue of the rich; there, in pandering to the caprices of society and the depraved tastes of the fashionable mob; there again, in forcing the consumer to buy what he does not need, or foisting an inferior article upon him by means of puffery, and in producing on the other hand wares which are absolutely injurious, but profitable to the manufacturer. What is squandered in this manner would be enough to double the production of useful things, or so to plenish our mills and factories with machinery that they would soon flood the shops with all that is now lacking to two-thirds of the nation. Under our present system a full quarter of the producers in every nation are forced to be idle for three or four months in the year, and the labour of another quarter, if not of the half, has no better results than the amusement of the rich or the exploitation of the public.

Thus, if we consider on the one hand the rapidity with which civilized nations augment their powers of production, and on the other hand the limits set to that production, be it directly or indirectly, by existing conditions, we cannot but conclude that an economic system a trifle more reasonable would permit them to heap up in a few years so many useful products that they would be constrained to say – 'Enough! We have enough coal and bread and raiment! Let us rest and consider how best to use our powers, how best to employ our leisure.'

No, plenty for all is not a dream – though it was a dream indeed in those days when man, for all his pains, could hardly win a few bushels of wheat from an acre of land, and had to fashion by hand all the implements he used in agriculture and industry. Now it is no longer a dream, because man has invented a motor which, with a little iron and a few sacks of coal, gives him the mastery of a creature strong and docile as a horse, and capable of setting the most complicated machinery in motion.

But, if plenty for all is to become a reality, this immense capital – cities, houses, pastures, arable lands, factories, highways, education – must cease to be regarded as private property, for the monopolist to dispose of at his pleasure.

This rich endowment, painfully won, builded, fashioned, or invented by our ancestors, must become common property, so that the collective interests of men may gain from it the greatest good for all.

There must be *expropriation*. The well-being of all – the end; expropriation – the means.

II

Expropriation, such then is the problem which history has put before the men of the twentieth century: the return to communism in all that ministers to the well-being of man.

But this problem cannot be solved by means of

legislation. No one imagines that. The poor, as well as the rich, understand that neither the existing governments, nor any which might arise out of possible political changes, would be capable of finding such a solution. They feel the necessity of a social revolution; and both rich and poor recognize that this revolution is imminent, that it may break out in a few years.

A great change in thought has taken place during the last half of the nineteenth century; but suppressed, as it was, by the propertied classes, and denied its natural development, this new spirit must now break its bonds by violence and realize itself in a revolution.

Whence will the revolution come? How will it announce its coming? No one can answer these questions. The future is hidden. But those who watch and think do not misinterpret the signs: workers and exploiters, revolutionists and conservatives, thinkers and men of action, all feel that a revolution is at our doors.

Well, then – what are we going to do when the thunderbolt has fallen?

We have all been bent on studying the dramatic side of revolutions so much, and the practical work of revolutions so little, that we are apt to see only the stage effects, so to speak, of these great movements:

the fight of the first days; the barricades. But this fight, this first skirmish, is soon ended, and it is only after the breakdown of the old system that the real work of revolution can be said to begin.

Effete and powerless, attacked on all sides, the old rulers are soon swept away by the breath of insurrection. In a few days the middle-class monarchy of 1848 was no more, and while Louis Philippe was making good his escape in a cab, Paris had already forgotten her 'citizen king'. The government of Thiers disappeared, on the 18th of March, 1871, in a few hours, leaving Paris mistress of her destinies. Yet 1848 and 1871 were only insurrections. Before a popular revolution the masters of 'the old order' disappear with a surprising rapidity. Its upholders fly the country, to plot in safety elsewhere and to devise measures for their return.

The former government having disappeared, the army, hesitating before the tide of popular opinion, no longer obeys its commanders, who have also prudently decamped. The troops stand by without interfering, or join the rebels. The police, standing at ease, are uncertain whether to belabour the crowd, or to cry: 'Long live the commune!' while some retire to their quarters 'to await the pleasure of the new government'. Wealthy citizens pack their trunks and betake themselves to places of safety.

The people remain. This is how a revolution is ushered in.

In several large towns the commune is proclaimed. In the streets wander scores of thousands of men, and in the evening they crowd into improvised clubs, asking: 'What shall we do?' and ardently discuss public affairs. All take an interest in them; those who yesterday were quite indifferent are perhaps the most zealous. Everywhere there is plenty of goodwill and a keen desire to make victory certain. It is a time when acts of supreme devotion are occurring. The masses of the people are full of the desire of going forward.

All this is splendid, sublime; but still, it is not a revolution. Nay, it is only now that the work of the revolutionist begins.

Doubtless there will be acts of vengeance. The Watrins and the Thomases will pay the penalty of their unpopularity; but these are mere incidents of the struggle – not the revolution.

Socialist politicians, radicals, neglected geniuses of journalism, stump orators – both middle-class people and workmen – will hurry to the town hall, to the government offices, to take possession of the vacant seats. Some will decorate themselves with gold and silver lace to their hearts' content, admire themselves in ministerial mirrors, and study to give

orders with an air of importance appropriate to
their new position. How could they impress their
comrades of the office or the workshop without
having a red sash, an embroidered cap and magis-
terial gestures! Others will bury themselves in
official papers, trying, with the best of wills, to make
head or tail of them. They will indite laws and issue
high-flown worded decrees that nobody will take
the trouble to carry out – because revolution has
come.

To give themselves an authority which they have
not they will seek the sanction of old forms of government. They will take the names of 'Provisional
Government', 'Committee of Public Safety', 'Mayor',
'Governor of the Town Hall', 'Commissioner of Public Safety', and what not. Elected or acclaimed, they
will assemble in boards or in communal councils,
where men of ten or twenty different schools will
come together, representing – not as many 'private
chapels', as it is often said, but as many different con-
ceptions regarding the scope, the bearing and the
goal of the revolution. Possibilists, collectivists, radicals, Jacobins, Blanquists, will be thrust together,
and waste time in wordy warfare. Honest men will
be huddled together with the ambitious ones, whose
only dream is power and who spurn the crowd
whence they are sprung. All coming together with

diametrically opposed views, all forced to enter into ephemeral alliances, in order to create majorities that can but last a day. Wrangling, calling each other reactionaries, authoritarians and rascals, incapable of coming to an understanding on any serious measure, dragged into discussions about trifles, producing nothing better than bombastic proclamations; all giving themselves an awful importance while the real strength of the movement is in the streets.

All this may please those who like the stage, but it is not revolution. Nothing has been accomplished as yet.

And meanwhile the people suffer. The factories are idle, the workshops closed; trade is at a standstill. The worker does not even earn the meagre wage which was his before. Food goes up in price. With that heroic devotion which has always characterized them, and which in great crises reaches the sublime, the people will wait patiently. 'We place these three months of want at the service of the Republic,' they said in 1848, while 'their representatives' and the gentlemen of the new government, down to the meanest Jack-in-office, received their salary regularly.

The people suffer. With the childlike faith, with the good humour of the masses who believe in their leaders, they think that 'yonder', in the House, in the town hall, in the Committee of Public Safety, their welfare is being considered. But 'yonder' they are discussing everything under the sun except the welfare of the people. In 1793, while famine ravaged France and crippled the Revolution; whilst the people were reduced to the depths of misery, although the Champs Elysées were lined with luxurious carriages where women displayed their jewels and splendour, Robespierre was urging the Jacobins to discuss his treatise on the English Constitution. While the worker was suffering in 1848 from the general stoppage of trade, the Provisional Government and the National Assembly were wrangling over military pensions and prison labour, without troubling how the people managed to live during the terrible crisis. And could one cast a reproach at the Paris Commune, which was born beneath the Prussian cannon, and lasted only seventy days, it would be for this same error – this failure to understand that the Revolution could not triumph unless those who fought on its side were fed: that on fifteen pence a day a man cannot fight on the ramparts and at the same time support a family.

The people suffer and say: 'How is a way out of these difficulties to be found?'

III

It seems to us that there is only one answer to this question: we must recognize, and loudly proclaim, that everyone, whatever his grade in the old society, whether strong or weak, capable or incapable, has, before everything, *the right to live*, and that society is bound to share among all, without exception, the means of existence it has at its disposal. We must acknowledge this, and proclaim it aloud, and act up to it.

Affairs must be managed in such a way that from the first day of the revolution the worker shall know that a new era is opening before him; that henceforward none need crouch under the bridges, while palaces are hard by, none need fast in the midst of plenty, none need perish with cold near shops full of furs; that all is for all, in practice as well as in theory, and that at last, for the first time in history, a revolution has been accomplished which considers the *needs* of the people before schooling them in their *duties*.

This cannot be brought about by Acts of Parliament, but only by taking immediate and effective possession of all that is necessary to ensure the well-being of all; this is the only really scientific way of going to work, the only way which can be understood and desired by the mass of the people. We must take possession, in the name of the people, of the granaries, the shops full of clothing and the dwelling-houses. Nothing must be wasted. We must organize without delay a way to feed the hungry, to satisfy all wants, to meet all needs, to produce not for the special benefit of this one or that one, but so as to ensure to society as a whole its life and further development.

Enough of ambiguous words like 'the right to work', with which the people were misled in 1848, and which are still resorted to with the hope of misleading them. Let us have the courage to recognize that *well-being for all*, henceforward possible, must be realized.

When the workers claimed the right to work in 1848, national and municipal workshops were organized, and workmen were sent to drudge there at the rate of 1*s*. 8*d*. a day! When they asked the 'Organization of Labour', the reply was: 'Patience, friends, the government will see to it; meantime here is your 1*s*. 8*d*. Rest now, brave toiler, after your lifelong struggle for food!' And in the meantime the cannons were overhauled, the reserves called out, and the workers themselves disorganized by the many methods well known to the middle classes, till one fine day, in June, 1848, four months after the overthrow of the previous government, they were told to go and colonize Africa, or be shot down.

Very different will be the result if the workers claim the *right to well-being*! In claiming that right they claim the right to take possession of the wealth of the community – to take houses to dwell in according to the needs of each family; to socialize the stores of food and learn the meaning of plenty, after having known famine too well. They proclaim their right to all social wealth – fruit of the labour of past and present generations – and learn by its means to enjoy those higher pleasures of art and science which have too long been monopolized by the rich.

And while asserting their right to live in comfort, they assert, what is still more important, their right to decide for themselves what this comfort shall be, what must be produced to ensure it, and what discarded as no longer of value.

The 'right to well-being' means the possibility of living like human beings, and of bringing up children to be members of a society better than ours, whilst the 'right to work' only means the right to be always a wage-slave, a drudge, ruled over and exploited by the middle class of the future. The right to well-being is the social revolution, the right to work means nothing but the treadmill of commercialism. It is high time for the worker to assert his right to the common inheritance, and to enter into possession of it.

3 Anarchist Communism

I

Every society, on abolishing private property will be forced, we maintain, to organize itself on the lines of communistic anarchy. Anarchy leads to communism, and communism to anarchy, both alike being expressions of the predominant tendency in modern societies, the pursuit of equality.

Time was when a peasant family could consider the corn it sowed and reaped, or the woollen garments woven in the cottage, as the products of its own soil. But even then this way of looking at things was not quite correct. There were the roads and the bridges made in common, the swamps drained by common toil, the communal pastures enclosed by hedges which were kept in repair by each and all. If the looms for weaving or the dyes for colouring fabrics were improved by somebody, all profited; and even in those days a peasant family could not live alone, but was dependent in a thousand ways on the village or the commune.

But nowadays, in the present state of industry, when everything is interdependent, when each branch of production is knit up with all the rest, the attempt to claim an individualist origin for the products of industry is absolutely untenable. The astonishing perfection attained by the textile or mining industries in civilized countries is due to the simultaneous development of a thousand other industries, great and small, to the extension of the railroad system, to inter-oceanic navigation, to the manual skill of thousands of workers, to a certain standard of culture reached by the working classes as a whole – to the labours, in short, of men in every corner of the globe.

The Italians who died of cholera while making the Suez Canal, or of anchylosis in the St Gothard Tunnel, and the Americans mowed down by shot and shell while fighting for the abolition of slavery, have helped to develop the cotton industry in France and England, as well as the work-girls who languish in the factories of Manchester and Rouen, and the inventor who (following the suggestion of some worker) succeeds in improving the looms.

How, then, shall we estimate the share of each in the riches which *all* contribute to amass?

Looking at production from this general, synthetic point of view, we cannot hold with the collectivists that payment proportionate to the hours of labour rendered by each would be an ideal arrangement, or even a step in the right direction.

Without discussing whether exchange value of goods is really measured in existing societies by the amount of work necessary to produce it – according to the teaching of Adam Smith and Ricardo, in whose footsteps Marx has followed – suffice it to say here, leaving ourselves free to return to the subject later, that the collectivist ideal appears to us untenable in a society which considers the instruments of labour as a common inheritance. Starting from this principle, such a society would find itself forced from the very outset to abandon all forms of wages.

The mitigated individualism of the collectivist system certainly could not maintain itself alongside a partial communism – the socialization of land and the instruments of production. A new form of property requires a new form of remuneration. A new method of production cannot exist side by side with the old forms of consumption, any more than it can adapt itself to the old forms of political organization.

The wage system arises out of the individual ownership of the land and the instruments of labour. It was the necessary condition for the development of capitalist production, and will perish with it, in spite of the attempt to disguise it as 'profit-sharing'. The common possession of the instruments of labour must necessarily bring with it the enjoyment in common of the fruits of common labour.

We hold further that communism is not only desirable, but that existing societies, founded on individualism, *are inevitably impelled in the direction of communism*. The development of individualism during the last three centuries is explained by the efforts of the individual to protect himself from the tyranny of capital and of the state. For a time he imagined, and those who expressed his thought for him declared, that he could free himself entirely from the state and from society. 'By means of money,' he said, 'I can buy all that I need.' But the individual was on a wrong track, and modern history has taught him to recognize that, without the help of all, he can do nothing, although his strongboxes are full of gold.

In fact, along with this current of individualism, we find in all modern history a tendency, on the one hand, to retain all that remains of the partial communism of antiquity, and, on the other, to establish the communist principle in the thousand developments of modern life.

As soon as the communes of the tenth, eleventh

and twelfth centuries had succeeded in emancipat-
ing themselves from their lords, ecclesiastical or lay,
their communal labour and communal consumption began to extend and develop rapidly. The
township – and not private persons – freighted ships
and equipped expeditions, for the export of their
manufacture, and the benefit arising from the foreign trade did not accrue to individuals, but was
shared by all. At the outset, the townships also
bought provisions for all their citizens. Traces of
these institutions have lingered on into the nineteenth century, and the people piously cherish the
memory of them in their legends.

All that has disappeared. But the rural township
still struggles to preserve the last traces of this communism, and it succeeds – except when the state
throws its heavy sword into the balance.

Meanwhile new organizations, based on the same
principle – *to every man according to his needs* – spring
up under a thousand different forms; for without a
certain leaven of communism the present societies
could not exist. In spite of the narrowly egotistic turn
given to men's minds by the commercial system, the
tendency towards communism is constantly appear-
ing, and it influences our activities in a variety
of ways.

The bridges, for the use of which a toll was levied

in the old days, have become public property and are free to all; so are the high roads, except in the East, where a toll is still exacted from the traveller for every mile of his journey. Museums, free libraries, free schools, free meals for children; parks and gardens open to all; streets paved and lighted, free to all; water supplied to every house without measure or stint – all such arrangements are founded on the principle: 'Take what you need.'

The tramways and railways have already introduced monthly and annual season tickets, without limiting the number of journeys taken; and two nations, Hungary and Russia, have introduced on their railways the zone system, which permits the holder to travel five hundred or eight hundred miles for the same price. It is but a short step from that to a uniform charge, such as already prevails in the postal service. In all these innovations, and in a thousand others, the tendency is not to measure the individual consumption. One man wants to travel eight hundred miles, another five hundred. These are personal requirements. There is no sufficient reason why one should pay twice as much as the other because his need is twice as great. Such are the signs which appear even now in our individualist societies.

Moreover, there is a tendency, though still a feeble

one, to consider the needs of the individual, irrespective of his past or possible services to the community. We are beginning to think of society as a whole, each part of which is so intimately bound up with the others that a service rendered to one is a service rendered to all.

When you go into a public library – not indeed the National Library of Paris, but, say, into the British Museum or the Berlin Library – the librarian does not ask what services you have rendered to society before giving you the book, or the fifty books, which you require; he even comes to your assistance if you do not know how to manage the catalogue. By means of uniform credentials – and very often a contribution of work is preferred – the scientific society opens its museums, its gardens, its library, its laboratories and its annual conversaziones to each of its members, whether he be a Darwin or a simple amateur.

At St Petersburg, if you are elaborating an invention, you go into a special laboratory, where you are given a place, a carpenter's bench, a turning lathe, all the necessary tools and scientific instruments, provided only you know how to use them; and you are allowed to work there as long as you please. There are the tools; interest others in your idea; join with fellow workers skilled in various crafts, or work alone if you prefer it. Invent a flying machine, or invent nothing – that is your own affair. You are pursuing an idea – that is enough.

In the same way, those who man the lifeboat do not ask credentials from the crew of a sinking ship; they launch their boat, risk their lives in the raging waves, and sometimes perish, all to save men whom they do not even know. And what need to know them? 'They are human beings, and they need our aid – that is enough, that establishes their right – To the rescue!'

Thus we find a tendency, eminently communistic, springing up on all sides, and in various guises, in the very heart of theoretically individualist societies.

Suppose that one of our great cities, so egotistic in ordinary times, were visited tomorrow by some calamity – a siege, for instance – that same selfish city would decide that the first needs to satisfy were those of the children and the aged. Without asking what services they had rendered, or were likely to render to society, it would first of all feed them. Then the combatants would be cared for, irrespective of the courage or the intelligence which each had displayed, and thousands of men and women would outvie each other in unselfish devotion to the wounded.

This tendency exists, and is felt as soon as the most pressing needs of each are satisfied, and in proportion as the productive power of the race increases. It becomes an active force every time a great idea comes to oust the mean preoccupations of everyday life.

How can we doubt, then, that when the instruments of production are placed at the service of all, when business is conducted on communist principles, when labour, having recovered its place of honour in society, produces much more than is necessary to all – how can we doubt that this force (already so powerful) will enlarge its sphere of action till it becomes the ruling principle of social life?

Following these indications, and considering further the practical side of expropriation, of which we shall speak in the following chapters, we are convinced that our first obligation, when the revolution shall have broken the power upholding the present system, will be to realize communism without delay.

But ours is neither the communism of Fourier and the phalansterians, nor of the German state socialists. It is anarchist communism, communism without government – the communism of the free. It is the synthesis of the two ideals pursued by humanity throughout the ages – economic and political liberty.

II

In taking 'anarchy' for our ideal of political organization we are only giving expression to another marked tendency of human progress. Whenever European societies have developed up to a certain point, they have shaken off the yoke of authority and substituted a system founded more or less on the principles of individual liberty. And history shows us that these periods of partial or general revolution, when the old governments were overthrown, were also periods of sudden progress in both the economic and the intellectual field. So it was after the enfranchisement of the communes, whose monuments, produced by the free labour of the guilds, have never been surpassed; so it was after the great peasant uprising which brought about the Reformation and imperilled the papacy; and so it was again with the society, free for a brief space, which was created on the other side of the Atlantic by the malcontents from the Old World.

And, if we observe the present development of civilized nations, we see, most unmistakably, a movement ever more and more marked tending to limit the sphere of action of the government, and to allow more and more liberty to the individual. This evolution is going on before our eyes, though cumbered by the ruins and rubbish of old institutions and old superstitions. Like all evolutions, it only awaits a revolution to overthrow the old obstacles which block the way, that it may find free scope in a regenerated society.

After having striven long in vain to solve the insoluble problem – the problem of constructing a government 'which will constrain the individual to obedience without itself ceasing to be the servant of society', men at last attempt to free themselves from every form of government and to satisfy their need for organization by free contracts between individuals and groups pursuing the same aim. The independence of each small territorial unit becomes a pressing need; mutual agreement replaces law in order to regulate individual interests in view of a common object – very often disregarding the frontiers of the present states.

All that was once looked on as a function of the government is today called in question. Things are arranged more easily and more satisfactorily without the intervention of the state. And in studying the progress made in this direction, we are led to conclude that the tendency of the human race is to reduce government interference to zero; in fact, to abolish the state, the personification of injustice, oppression and monopoly.

We can already catch glimpses of a world in which the bonds which bind the individual are no longer laws, but social habits – the result of the need felt by each one of us to seek the support, the co-operation, the sympathy of his neighbours.

Assuredly the idea of a society without a state will give rise to at least as many objections as the political economy of a society without private capital. We have all been brought up from our childhood to regard the state as a sort of providence; all our education, the Roman history we learned at school, the Byzantine code which we studied later under the name of Roman law, and the various sciences taught at the universities, accustom us to believe in government and in the virtues of the state providential.

To maintain this superstition whole systems of philosophy have been elaborated and taught; all politics are based on this principle; and each politician, whatever his colours, comes forward and says to the people, 'Give my party the power; we can and we will free you from the miseries which press so heavily upon you.'

From the cradle to the grave all our actions are guided by this principle. Open any book on sociology

or jurisprudence, and you will find there the government, its organization, its acts, filling so large a place
that we come to believe that there is nothing outside
the government and the world of statesmen.

The press teaches us the same in every conceivable
way. Whole columns are devoted to parliamentary
debates and to political intrigues; while the vast
everyday life of a nation appears only in the columns
given to economic subjects, or in the pages devoted
to reports of police and law cases. And when you
read the newspapers, you hardly think of the in-
calculable number of beings – all humanity, so to
say – who grow up and die, who know sorrow, who
work and consume, think and create outside the few
encumbering personages who have been so magni-
fied that humanity is hidden by their shadows,
enlarged by our ignorance.

And yet as soon as we pass from printed matter to
life itself, as soon as we throw a glance at society, we
are struck by the infinitesimal part played by the
government. Balzac already remarked how millions
of peasants spend the whole of their lives without
knowing anything about the state, save the heavy
taxes they are compelled to pay. Every day millions
of transactions are made without government
intervention, and the greatest of them – those of
commerce and of the Exchange – are carried on in

such a way that the government could not be appealed to if one of the contracting parties had the intention of not fulfilling his agreement. Should you speak to a man who understands commerce, he will tell you that the everyday business transacted by merchants would be absolutely impossible were it not based on mutual confidence. The habit of keeping his word, the desire not to lose his credit, amply suffice to maintain this relative honesty. The man who does not feel the slightest remorse when poisoning his customers with noxious drugs covered with pompous labels, thinks he is in honour bound to keep his engagements. But if this relative morality has developed under present conditions, when enrichment is the only incentive and the only aim, can we doubt its rapid progress when appropriation of the fruits of others' labour will no longer be the basis of society?

Another striking fact, which especially characterizes our generation, speaks still more in favour of our ideas. It is the continual extension of the field of enterprise due to private initiative, and the prodigious development of free organizations of all kinds. We shall discuss this more at length in the chapter devoted to 'Free Agreement'. Suffice it to mention that the facts are so numerous and so customary that they are the essence of the second half of the nineteenth century, even though political and socialist writers ignore them, always preferring to talk to us about the functions of the government.

These organizations, free and infinitely varied, are so natural an outcome of our civilization; they expand so rapidly and federate with so much ease; they are so necessary a result of the continual growth of the needs of civilized man; and lastly, they so advantageously replace governmental interference, that we must recognize in them a factor of growing importance in the life of societies. If they do not yet spread over the whole of the manifestations of life, it is that they find an insurmountable obstacle in the poverty of the worker, in the divisions of present society, in the private appropriation of capital, and in the state. Abolish these obstacles, and you will see them covering the immense field of civilized man's activity.

The history of the last fifty years furnishes a living proof that representative government is impotent to discharge all the functions we have sought to assign to it. In days to come the nineteenth century will be quoted as having witnessed the failure of parliamentarianism.

This impotence is becoming so evident to all; the faults of parliamentarianism, and the inherent vices of the representative principle, are so self-evident that the few thinkers who have made a critical study of them (J. S. Mill, Leverdays) did but give literary form to the popular dissatisfaction. It is not difficult, indeed, to see the absurdity of naming a few men and saying to them, 'Make laws regulating all our spheres of activity, although not one of you knows anything about them!'

We are beginning to see that government by majorities means abandoning all the affairs of the country to the tide-waiters who make up the majorities in the House and in election committees; to those, in a word, who have no opinion of their own.

Mankind is seeking and already finding new issues. The International Postal Union, the railway unions and the learned societies give us examples of solutions based on free agreement in place and stead of law.

Today, when groups scattered far and wide wish to organize themselves for some object or other, they no longer elect an international parliament of Jacks-of-all-trades. They proceed in a different way. Where it is not possible to meet directly or come to an agreement by correspondence, delegates versed in the question at issue are sent, and they are told: 'Endeavour to come to an agreement on such or such a question, and then return, not with a law in your pocket, but with a proposition of agreement which we may or may not accept.'

Such is the method of the great industrial companies, the learned societies and numerous associations of every description, which already cover Europe and the United States. And such will be the method of a free society. A society founded on serfdom is in keeping with absolute monarchy; a society based on the wage system and the exploitation of the masses by the capitalists finds its political expression in parliamentarianism. But a free society, regaining possession of the common inheritance, must seek, in free groups and free federations of groups, a new organization, in harmony with the new economic phase of history.

Every economic phase has a political phase corresponding to it, and it would be impossible to touch private property unless a new mode of political life be found at the same time.

4 *Expropriation*

It is told of Rothschild that, seeing his fortune threatened by the revolution of 1848, he hit upon the following stratagem: 'I am quite willing to admit,' said he, 'that my fortune has been accumulated at the expense of others; but if it were divided tomorrow among the millions of Europe, the share of each would only amount to four shillings. Very well, then, I undertake to render to each his four shillings if he asks me for it.'

Having given due publicity to his promise, our millionaire proceeded as usual to stroll quietly through the streets of Frankfort. Three or four passers-by asked for their four shillings, which he disbursed with a sardonic smile. His stratagem succeeded, and the family of the millionaire is still in possession of its wealth.

It is in much the same fashion that the shrewd heads among the middle classes reason when they say, 'Ah, expropriation! I know what that means. You take all the overcoats and lay them in a heap, and everyone is free to help himself and fight for the best.'

But such jests are irrelevant as well as flippant. What we want is not a redistribution of overcoats, although it must be said that even in such a case, the shivering folk would see advantage in it. Nor do we want to divide up the wealth of the Rothschilds. What we do want is so to arrange things that every human being born into the world shall be ensured the opportunity, in the first instance of learning some useful occupation, and of becoming skilled in it; and next, that he shall be free to work at his trade without asking leave of master or owner, and without handing over to landlord or capitalist the lion's share of what he produces. As to the wealth held by the Rothschilds or the Vanderbilts, it will serve us to organize our system of communal production.

The day when the labourer may till the ground without paying away half of what he produces, the day when the machines necessary to prepare the soil for rich harvests are at the free disposal of the cultivators, the day when the worker in the factory produces for the community and not the monopolist – that day will see the workers clothed and fed, and there will be no more Rothschilds or other exploiters.

No one will then have to sell his working power for a wage that only represents a fraction of what he produces.

'So far so good,' say our critics, 'but you will have Rothschilds coming in from outside. How are you to prevent a person from amassing millions in China, and then settling among you? How are you going to prevent such a one from surrounding himself with lackeys and wage-slaves – from exploiting them and enriching himself at their expense?

'You cannot bring about a revolution all over the world at the same time. Well, then – are you going to establish custom-houses on your frontiers to search all who enter your country and confiscate the money they bring with them? – Anarchist policemen firing on travellers would be a fine spectacle!'

But at the root of this argument there is a great error. Those who propound it have never paused to enquire whence come the fortunes of the rich. A little thought would, however, suffice to show them that these fortunes have their beginnings in the poverty of the poor. When there are no longer any destitute, there will no longer be any rich to exploit them.

Let us glance for a moment at the Middle Ages, when great fortunes began to spring up.

A feudal baron seizes on a fertile valley. But as long as the fertile valley is empty of folk our baron is not rich. His land brings him in nothing; he might as well possess a property in the moon.

What does our baron do to enrich himself? He looks out for peasants – for poor peasants!

If every peasant-farmer had a piece of land, free from rent and taxes, if he had in addition the tools and the stock necessary for farm labour – who would plough the lands of the baron? Everyone would look after his own. But there are thousands of destitute persons ruined by wars, or drought, or pestilence. They have neither horse nor plough. (Iron was very costly in the Middle Ages, and a draught-horse still more so.)

All these destitute creatures are trying to better their condition. One day they see on the road at the confines of our baron's estate a notice-board indicating by certain signs adapted to their comprehension that the labourer who is willing to settle on this estate will receive the tools and materials to build his cottage and sow his fields, and a portion of land rent free for a certain number of years. The number of years is represented by so many crosses on the signboard, and the peasant understands the meaning of these crosses.

So the poor wretches come to settle on the baron's lands. They make roads, drain the marshes, build villages. In nine or ten years the baron begins to tax them. Five years later he increases the rent. Then he doubles it, and the peasant accepts these new conditions because he cannot find better ones elsewhere. Little by little, with the aid of laws made by the barons, the poverty of the peasant becomes the source of the landlord's wealth. And it is not only the lord of the manor who preys upon him. A whole host of usurers swoop down upon the villages, multiplying as the wretchedness of the peasants increases. That is how these things happened in the Middle Ages. And today is it not still the same thing? If there were free lands which the peasant could cultivate if he pleased, would he pay £50 to some 'shabble of a duke'* for condescending to sell him a scrap? Would he burden himself with a lease which absorbed a third of the produce? Would he – on the *métayer* system – consent to give the half of his harvest to the landowner?

But he has nothing. So he will accept any

---

* 'Shabble of a duke' is an expression coined by Carlyle; it is a somewhat free rendering of Kropotkin's 'Monsieur le Vicomte', but I think it expresses his meaning. – *Trans.*

conditions, if only he can keep body and soul together, while he tills the soil and enriches the landlord.

So in the nineteenth century, just as in the Middle Ages, the poverty of the peasant is a source of wealth to the landed proprietor.

II

The landlord owes his riches to the poverty of the peasants, and the wealth of the capitalist comes from the same source.

Take the case of a citizen of the middle class, who somehow or other finds himself in possession of £20,000. He could, of course, spend his money at the rate of £2,000 a year, a mere bagatelle in these days of fantastic, senseless luxury. But then he would have nothing left at the end of ten years. So, being a 'practical person', he prefers to keep his fortune intact, and win for himself a snug little annual income as well.

This is very easy in our society, for the good reason that the towns and villages swarm with workers who have not the wherewithal to live for a month, or even a fortnight. So our worthy citizen starts a factory. The banks hasten to lend him another £20,000, especially if he has a reputation for 'business ability'; and with this round sum he can command the labour of five hundred hands.

If all the men and women in the countryside had their daily bread assured, and their daily needs already satisfied, who would work for our capitalist at a wage of half a crown a day, while the commodities one produces in a day sell in the market for a crown or more?

Unhappily – we know it all too well – the poor quarters of our towns and the neighbouring villages are full of needy wretches, whose children clamour for bread. So, before the factory is well finished, the workers hasten to offer themselves. Where a hundred are required three hundred besiege the doors, and from the time his mill is started, the owner, if he only has average business capacities, will clear £40 a year out of each mill-hand he employs.

He is thus able to lay by a snug little fortune; and if he chooses a lucrative trade, and has 'business talents', he will soon increase his income by doubling the number of the men he exploits.

So he becomes a personage of importance. He can afford to give dinners to other personages – to the local magnates, the civic, legal and political dignitaries. With his money he can 'marry money'; by and by he may pick and choose places for his children, and later on perhaps get something good from the government – a contract for the army or for the police. His gold breeds gold; till at last a war, or even a rumour of war, or a speculation on the Stock Exchange, gives him his great opportunity.

Nine-tenths of the great fortunes made in the United States are (as Henry George has shown in his *Social Problems*) the result of knavery on a large scale, assisted by the state. In Europe, nine-tenths of the fortunes made in our monarchies and republics have the same origin. There are not two ways of becoming a millionaire.

This is the secret of wealth: find the starving and destitute, pay them half a crown, and make them produce five shillings' worth in the day, amass a fortune by these means, and then increase it by some lucky speculation, made with the help of the state.

Need we go on to speak of small fortunes attributed by the economists to forethought and frugality, when we know that mere saving in itself brings in nothing, so long as the pence saved are not used to exploit the famishing?

Take a shoemaker, for instance. Grant that his work is well paid, that he has plenty of custom, and that by dint of strict frugality he contrives to lay by from eighteen pence to two shillings a day, perhaps two pounds a month.

Grant that our shoemaker is never ill; that he does

not half starve himself, in spite of his passion for economy; that he does not marry or that he has no children; that he does not die of consumption; suppose anything and everything you please!

Well, at the age of fifty he will not have scraped together £800; and he will not have enough to live on during his old age, when he is past work. Assuredly this is not how fortunes are made. But suppose our shoemaker, as soon as he has laid by a few pence, thriftily conveys them to the savings bank, and that the savings bank lends them to the capitalist who is just about to 'employ labour', i.e., to exploit the poor. Then our shoemaker takes an apprentice, the child of some poor wretch, who will think himself lucky if in five years' time his son has learned the trade and is able to earn his living.

Meanwhile our shoemaker does not lose by him, and if trade is brisk he soon takes a second, and then a third apprentice. By and by he will take two or three working men – poor wretches, thankful to receive half a crown a day for work that is worth five shillings, and if our shoemaker is 'in luck', that is to say, if he is keen enough and mean enough, his working men and apprentices will bring him in nearly one pound a day, over and above the product of his own toil. He can then enlarge his business. He will gradually become rich, and no longer have any need to stint himself in the necessaries of life. He will leave a snug little fortune to his son.

That is what people call 'being economical and having frugal, temperate habits'. At bottom it is nothing more nor less than grinding the face of the poor.

Commerce seems an exception to this rule. 'Such a man,' we are told, 'buys tea in China, brings it to France, and realizes a profit of 30 per cent on his original outlay. He has exploited nobody.'

Nevertheless, the case is quite similar. If our merchant had carried his bales on his back, well and good! In early medieval times that was exactly how foreign trade was conducted, and so no one reached such giddy heights of fortune as in our days. Very few and very hardly earned were the gold coins which the medieval merchant gained from a long and dangerous voyage. It was less the love of money than the thirst of travel and adventure that inspired his undertakings.

Nowadays the method is simpler. A merchant who has some capital need not stir from his desk to become wealthy. He telegraphs to an agent telling him to buy a hundred tons of tea; he freights a ship, and in a few weeks, in three months if it is a sailing ship, the vessel brings him his cargo. He does not even take the risks of the voyage, for his tea and his vessel are insured, and if he has expended four thousand pounds he will receive more than five or six thousand; that is to say, if he has not attempted to speculate in some novel commodities, in which case he runs a chance of either doubling his fortune or losing it altogether.

Now, how could he find men willing to cross the sea, to travel to China and back, to endure hardship and slavish toil and to risk their lives for a miserable pittance? How could he find dock labourers willing to load and unload his ships for 'starvation wages'? How? Because they are needy and starving. Go to the seaports, visit the cook-shops and taverns on the quays, and look at these men who have come to hire themselves, crowding round the dock gates, which they besiege from early dawn, hoping to be allowed to work on the vessels. Look at these sailors, happy to be hired for a long voyage, after weeks and months of waiting. All their lives long they have gone to the sea in ships, and they will sail in others still, until they have perished in the waves.

Enter their homes, look at their wives and children in rags, living one knows not how till the father's return, and you will have the answer to the question.

Multiply examples, choose them where you will, consider the origin of all fortunes, large or small, whether arising out of commerce, finance, manufactures or the land. Everywhere you will find that the wealth of the wealthy springs from the poverty of the poor. This is why an anarchist society need not fear the advent of a Rothschild who would settle in its midst. If every member of the community knows that after a few hours of productive toil he will have a right to all the pleasures that civilization procures, and to those deeper sources of enjoyment which art and science offer to all who seek them, he will not sell his strength for a starvation wage. No one will volunteer to work for the enrichment of your Rothschild. His golden guineas will be only so many pieces of metal – useful for various purposes, but incapable of breeding more.

In answering the above objection we have at the same time indicated the scope of expropriation. It must apply to everything that enables any man – be he financier, mill-owner, or landlord – to appropriate the product of others' toil. Our formula is simple and comprehensive.

We do not want to rob anyone of his coat, but we wish to give to the workers all those things the lack of which makes them fall an easy prey to the exploiter, and we will do our utmost that none shall lack aught, that not a single man shall be forced to sell the strength of his right arm to obtain a bare subsistence for himself and his babes. This is what we mean when we talk of expropriation; this will be our duty during the revolution, for whose coming we look, not two hundred years hence, but soon, very soon.

The ideas of anarchism in general and of expropriation in particular find much more sympathy than we are apt to imagine among men of independent character, and those for whom idleness is not the supreme ideal. 'Still,' our friends often warn us, 'take care you do not go too far! Humanity cannot be changed in a day, so do not be in too great a hurry with your schemes of expropriation and anarchy, or you will be in danger of achieving no permanent result.'

Now, what we fear with regard to expropriation is exactly the contrary. We are afraid of not going far enough, of carrying out expropriation on too small a scale to be lasting. We would not have the revolutionary impulse arrested in mid-career, to exhaust itself in half measures, which would content no one, and while producing a tremendous confusion in society, and stopping its customary activities, would have no vital power – would merely spread general discontent and inevitably prepare the way for the triumph of reaction.

There are, in fact, in a modern state established relations which it is practically impossible to modify if one attacks them only in detail. There are wheels within wheels in our economic organization – the machinery is so complex and interdependent that no one part can be modified without disturbing the whole. This becomes clear as soon as an attempt is made to expropriate anything.

Let us suppose that in a certain country a limited form of expropriation is effected. For example, that, as it has been suggested more than once, only the property of the great landlords is socialized, whilst the factories are left untouched; or that, in a certain city, house property is taken over by the commune, but everything else is left to private ownership; or that, in some manufacturing centre, the factories are communalized, but the land is not interfered with.

The same result would follow in each case – a terrible shattering of the industrial system, without the means of reorganizing it on new lines. Industry and finance would be at a deadlock, yet a return to the first principles of justice would not have been achieved, and society would find itself powerless to construct a harmonious whole.

If agriculture were freed from great landowners,

while industry still remained the bond-slave of the capitalist, the merchant and the banker, nothing would be accomplished. The peasant suffers today not only in having to pay rent to the landlord; he is oppressed on all hands by existing conditions. He is exploited by the tradesman, who makes him pay half a crown for a spade which, measured by the labour spent on it, is not worth more than sixpence. He is taxed by the state, which cannot do without its formidable hierarchy of officials, and finds it necessary to maintain an expensive army, because the traders of all nations are perpetually fighting for the markets, and any day a little quarrel arising from the exploitation of some part of Asia or Africa may result in war.

Then again the peasant suffers from the depopulation of country places: the young people are attracted to the large manufacturing towns by the bait of high wages paid temporarily by the producers of articles of luxury, or by the attractions of a more stirring life. The artificial protection of industry, the industrial exploitation of foreign countries, the prevalence of stock-jobbing, the difficulty of improving the soil and the machinery of production – all these agencies combine nowadays to work against agriculture, which is burdened not only by rent, but by the whole complex of conditions in a society based on exploitation. Thus, even if the expropriation of land were accomplished, and everyone were free to till the soil and cultivate it to the best advantage, without paying rent, agriculture, even though it should enjoy – which can by no means be taken for granted – a momentary prosperity, would soon fall back into the slough in which it finds itself today. The whole thing would have to be begun over again, with increased difficulties.

The same holds true of industry. Take the converse case: instead of turning the agricultural labourers into peasant-proprietors, make over the factories to those who work in them. Abolish the master-manufacturers, but leave the landlord his land, the banker his money, the merchant his Exchange; maintain the swarm of idlers who live on the toil of the workmen, the thousand and one middlemen, the state with its numberless officials – and industry would come to a standstill. Finding no purchasers in the mass of peasants who would remain poor; not possessing the raw material, and unable to export their produce, partly on account of the stoppage of trade, and still more so because industries spread all over the world, the manufacturers would feel unable to struggle, and thousands of workers would be thrown upon the streets. These starving crowds would be ready and willing to submit to the first schemer who came to exploit them; they would even consent to return to the old slavery, under promise of guaranteed work.

Or, finally, suppose you oust the landowners, and hand over the mills and factories to the workers, without interfering with the swarm of middlemen who drain the product of our manufacturers, and speculate in corn and flour, meat and groceries, in our great centres of commerce. Then, as soon as the exchange of produce is slackened; as soon as the great cities are left without bread, while the great manufacturing centres find no buyers for the articles of luxury they produce, the counter-revolution is bound to take place, and it would come, treading upon the slain, sweeping the towns and villages with shot and shell; indulging in orgies of proscriptions and deportations, such as were seen in France in 1815, 1848 and 1871.

All is interdependent in a civilized society; it is impossible to reform any one thing without altering the whole. Therefore, on the day a nation will strike at private property, under any one of its forms, territorial or industrial, it will be obliged to attack them all. The very success of the revolution will impose it.

Besides, even if it were desired, it would be impossible to confine the change to a partial expropriation.

Once the principle of the 'divine right of property' is shaken, no amount of theorizing will prevent its overthrow, here by the slaves of the field, there by the slaves of the machine.

If a great town, Paris for example, were to confine itself to taking possession of the dwelling-houses or the factories, it would be forced also to deny the right of the bankers to levy upon the commune a tax amounting to £2,000,000, in the form of interest for former loans. The great city would be obliged to put itself in touch with the rural districts, and its influence would inevitably urge the peasants to free themselves from the landowner. It would be necessary to communalize the railways, that the citizens might get food and work, and lastly, to prevent the waste of supplies, and to guard against the trusts of corn-speculators, like those to whom the Paris Commune of 1793 fell a prey, it would have to place in the hands of the city the work of stocking its warehouses with commodities, and apportioning the produce.

Some socialists still seek, however, to establish a distinction. 'Of course,' they say, 'the soil, the mines, the mills and manufactures must be expropriated, these are the instruments of production, and it is right we should consider them public property. But articles of consumption – food, clothes and dwellings – should remain private property.'

Popular common sense has got the better of this subtle distinction. We are not savages who can live in the woods, without other shelter than the branches. The civilized man needs a roof, a room, a hearth and a bed. It is true that the bed, the room and the house is a home of idleness for the non-producer. But for the worker, a room, properly heated and lighted, is as much an instrument of production as the tool or the machine. It is the place where the nerves and sinews gather strength for the work of the morrow. The rest of the workman is the daily repairing of the machine.

The same argument applies even more obviously to food. The so-called economists, who make the just-mentioned distinction, would hardly deny that the coal burnt in a machine is as necessary to production as the raw material itself. How then can food, without which the human machine could do no work, be excluded from the list of things indispensable to the producer? Can this be a relic of religious metaphysics? The rich man's feast is indeed a matter of luxury, but the food of the worker is just as much a part of production as the fuel burnt by the steam-engine.

The same with clothing. We are not New Guinea savages. And if the dainty gowns of our ladies must rank as objects of luxury, there is nevertheless a certain quantity of linen, cotton and woollen stuff which is a necessity of life to the producer. The shirt and trousers in which he goes to his work, the jacket he slips on after the day's toil is over, are as necessary to him as the hammer to the anvil.

Whether we like it or not, this is what the people mean by a revolution. As soon as they have made a clean sweep of the government, they will seek first of all to ensure to themselves decent dwellings and sufficient food and clothes – free of capitalist rent.

And the people will be right. The methods of the people will be much more in accordance with science than those of the economists who draw so many distinctions between instruments of production and articles of consumption. The people understand that this is just the point where the revolution ought to begin; and they will lay the foundations of the only economic science worthy the name – a science which might be called: 'The Study of the Needs of Humanity, and of the Economic Means to Satisfy Them'.

5 *Food*

I

If the coming revolution is to be a social revolution, it will be distinguished from all former uprisings not only by its aim, but also by its methods. To attain a new end, new means are required.

The three great popular movements which we have seen in France during the last hundred years differ from each other in many ways, but they have one common feature.

In each case the people strove to overturn the old regime, and spent their heart's blood for the cause. Then, after having borne the brunt of the battle, they sank again into obscurity. A government, composed of men more or less honest, was formed and undertook to organize a new regime: the Republic in 1793, Labour in 1848, the Free Commune in 1871. Imbued with Jacobin ideas, the government occupied itself first of all with political questions, such as the reorganization of the machinery of government, the purifying of the administration, the separation of church and state, civic liberty, and such matters. It is true the workmen's clubs kept an eye on the members of the new government, and often imposed their ideas on them. But even in these clubs, whether the leaders belonged to the middle or to the working classes, it was always middle-class ideas which prevailed. They discussed various political questions at great length, but forgot to discuss the question of bread.

Great ideas sprang up at such times, ideas that have moved the world; words were spoken which still stir our hearts, at the interval of more than a century. But the people were starving in the slums.

From the very commencement of the Revolution industry inevitably came to a stop – the circulation of produce was checked, and capital concealed itself. The master – the employer – had nothing to fear at such times, he battened on his dividends, if indeed he did not speculate on the wretchedness around; but the wage-earner was reduced to live from hand to mouth. Want knocked at the door.

Famine was abroad in the land – such famine as had hardly been seen under the old regime.

'The Girondists are starving us!' was the cry in the workmen's quarters in 1793, and thereupon the Girondists were guillotined, and full powers were given to 'the Mountain' and to the Commune. The Commune indeed concerned itself with the question of bread, and made heroic efforts to feed Paris. At Lyons, Fouché and Collot d'Herbois established city granaries, but the sums spent on filling them were woefully insufficient. The town councils made great efforts to procure corn; the bakers who hoarded flour were hanged – and still the people lacked bread.

Then they turned on the royalist conspirators and laid the blame at their door. They guillotined a dozen or fifteen a day – servants and duchesses alike, especially servants, for the duchesses had gone to Koblenz. But if they had guillotined a hundred dukes and viscounts every day, it would have been equally hopeless.

The want only grew. For the wage-earner cannot live without his wage, and the wage was not forthcoming. What difference could a thousand corpses more or less make to him?

Then the people began to grow weary. 'So much for your vaunted Revolution! You are more wretched than ever before,' whispered the reactionary in the ears of the worker. And little by little the rich took courage, emerged from their hiding-places, and flaunted their luxury in the face of the starving multitude. They dressed up like scented fops and said to the workers: 'Come, enough of this foolery! What have you gained by your Revolution?'

And, sick at heart, his patience at an end, the revolutionary had at last to admit to himself that the cause was lost once more. He retreated into his hovel and awaited the worst.

Then reaction proudly asserted itself, and accomplished a counter-revolutionary stroke. The Revolution dead, nothing remained but to trample its corpse under foot.

The White Terror began. Blood flowed like water, the guillotine was never idle, the prisons were crowded, while the pageant of rank and fashion resumed its old course, and went on as merrily as before.

This picture is typical of all our revolutions. In 1848 the workers of Paris placed 'three months of starvation' at the service of the Republic, and then, having reached the limit of their powers, they made, in June, one last desperate effort – an effort which was drowned in blood. In 1871 the Commune perished for lack of combatants. It had taken measures for the separation of church and state, but it neglected, alas, until too late, to take measures for providing the people with bread. And so it came to pass in Paris that *élégantes* and fine gentlemen could spurn the confederates, and bid them go sell their lives for a miserable pittance, and leave their 'betters' to feast at their ease in fashionable restaurants.

At last the Commune saw its mistake, and opened communal kitchens. But it was too late. Its days were already numbered, and the troops of Versailles were on the ramparts.

'Bread, it is bread that the revolution needs!'

Let others spend their time in issuing pompous proclamations, in decorating themselves lavishly with official gold lace, and in talking about political liberty! . . .

Be it ours to see, from the first day of the revolution to the last, in all the provinces fighting for freedom, that there is not a single man who lacks bread, not a single woman compelled to stand with the wearied crowd outside the bakehouse-door, that haply a coarse loaf may be thrown to her in charity, not a single child pining for want of food.

It has always been the middle-class idea to harangue about 'great principles' – great lies rather!

The idea of the people will be to provide bread for all. And while middle-class citizens, and workmen infested with middle-class ideas, admire their own rhetoric in the 'talking shops', and 'practical people' are engaged in endless discussions on forms of government, we, the 'utopian dreamers' – we shall have to consider the question of daily bread.

We have the temerity to declare that all have a

right to bread, that there is bread enough for all, and that with this watchword of *Bread for All* the revolution will triumph.

II

That we are utopians is well known. So utopian are we that we go the length of believing that the revolution can and ought to assure shelter, food and clothes to all – an idea extremely displeasing to middle-class citizens, whatever their party colour, for they are quite alive to the fact that it is not easy to keep the upper hand of a people whose hunger is satisfied.

All the same, we maintain our contention: bread must be found for the people of the revolution, and the question of bread must take precedence over all other questions. If it is settled in the interests of the people, the revolution will be on the right road; for in solving the question of bread we must accept the principle of equality, which will force itself upon us to the exclusion of every other solution.

It is certain that the coming revolution – like in that respect to the revolution of 1848 – will burst upon us in the middle of a great industrial crisis. Things have been seething for half a century now, and can only go from bad to worse. Everything tends that way – new nations entering the lists of international trade and fighting for possession of the world's markets, wars, taxes ever increasing. National debts, the insecurity of the morrow, and huge colonial undertakings in every corner of the globe.

There are millions of unemployed workers in Europe at this moment. It will be still worse when revolution has burst upon us and spread like fire laid to a train of gunpowder. The number of the out-of-works will be doubled as soon as barricades are erected in Europe and the United States. What is to be done to provide these multitudes with bread?

We do not know whether the folk who call themselves 'practical people' have ever asked themselves this question in all its nakedness. But we do know that they wish to maintain the wage system, and we must therefore expect to have 'national workshops' and 'public works' vaunted as a means of giving food to the unemployed.

Because national workshops were opened in 1789 and 1793; because the same means were resorted to in 1848; because Napoleon III succeeded in contenting the Parisian proletariat for eighteen years by giving them public works – which cost Paris today its debt of £80,000,000, and its municipal tax of three

or four pounds a head;* because this excellent
method of 'taming the beast' was customary in
Rome, and even in Egypt four thousand years ago;
and lastly, because despots, kings and emperors have
always employed the ruse of throwing a scrap of
food to the people to gain time to snatch up the
whip – it is natural that 'practical' men should extol
this method of perpetuating the wage system. What
need to rack our brains when we have the time-
honoured method of the Pharaohs at our disposal?

Yet should the revolution be so misguided as to
start on this path, it would be lost.

In 1848, when the national workshops were
opened on 27 February, the unemployed of Paris
numbered only 8,000; a fortnight later they had
already increased to 49,000. They would soon have
been 100,000, without counting those who crowded
in from the provinces.

Yet at that time trade and manufactures in France
employed half as many hands as today. And we
know that in time of revolution exchange and industry suffer most from the general upheaval. We have
only to think, indeed, of the number of workmen

---

* The municipal debt of Paris amounted in 1904 to
2,266,579,100 francs, and the charges for it were
121,000,000 francs.

whose labour depends directly or indirectly upon export trade, or of the number of hands employed in producing luxuries, whose consumers are the middle-class minority.

A revolution in Europe means, then, the unavoidable stoppage of at least half the factories and workshops. It means millions of workers and their families thrown on the streets. And our 'practical men' would seek to avert this truly terrible situation by means of national relief works; that is to say, by means of new industries created on the spot to give work to the unemployed!

It is evident, as Proudhon had already pointed out more than fifty years ago, that the smallest attack upon property will bring in its train the complete disorganization of the system based upon private enterprise and wage labour. Society itself will be forced to take production in hand, in its entirety, and to reorganize it to meet the needs of the whole people. But this cannot be accomplished in a day, or even in a month; it must take a certain time to reorganize the system of production, and during this time millions of men will be deprived of the means of subsistence. What then is to be done?

There is only one really *practical* solution of the problem – boldly to face the great task which awaits us, and instead of trying to patch up a situation which we ourselves have made untenable, to proceed to reorganize production on a new basis.

Thus the really practical course of action, in our view, would be that the people should take immediate possession of all the food of the insurgent communes, keeping strict account of it all, that none might be wasted, and that by the aid of these accumulated resources everyone might be able to tide over the crisis. During that time an agreement would have to be made with the factory workers, the necessary raw material given them, and the means of subsistence assured to them, while they worked to supply the needs of the agricultural population. For we must not forget that while France weaves silks and satins to deck the wives of German financiers, the Empress of Russia and the Queen of the Sandwich Islands, and while Paris fashions wonderful trinkets and playthings for rich folk all the world over, two-thirds of the French peasantry have not proper lamps to give them light, or the implements necessary for modern agriculture. Lastly, unproductive land, of which there is plenty, would have to be turned to the best advantage, poor soils enriched, and rich soils, which yet, under the present system, do not yield a quarter, no, nor a tenth of what they might produce, would be submitted to intensive culture, and tilled with as much care as a market garden or a flower plot. It is impossible to imagine any other practical solution of the problem; and, whether we like it or not, sheer force of circumstances will bring it to pass.

III

The most prominent characteristic of our present capitalism is *the wage system*, which in brief amounts to this:

A man, or a group of men, possessing the necessary capital, starts some industrial enterprise; he undertakes to supply the factory or workshops with raw material, to organize production, to pay the employees a fixed wage, and lastly, to pocket the surplus value or profits, under pretext of recouping himself for managing the concern, for running the risks it may involve, and for the fluctuations of price in the market value of the wares.

To preserve this system, those who now monopolize capital would be ready to make certain concessions; to share, for example, a part of the profits with the workers, or rather to establish a 'sliding scale', which would oblige them to raise wages when prices were high; in brief, they would consent to certain sacrifices on condition that they were still allowed to direct industry and to take its first fruits.

Collectivism, as we know, does not abolish the wage system, though it introduces considerable modifications into the existing order of things. It only substitutes the state, that is to say, some form of representative government, national or local, for the individual employer of labour. Under collectivism it is the representatives of the nation, or of the commune, and their deputies and officials who are to have the control of industry. It is they who reserve to themselves the right of employing the surplus of production – in the interests of all. Moreover, collectivism draws a very subtle but very far-reaching distinction between the work of the labourer and of the man who has learned a craft. Unskilled labour in the eyes of the collectivist is *simple* labour, while the work of the craftsman, the mechanic, the engineer, the man of science, etc., is what Marx calls *complex* labour, and is entitled to a higher wage. But labourers and craftsmen, weavers and men of science, are all wage-servants of the state – 'all officials', as was said lately, to gild the pill.

Well, then, the coming revolution could render no greater service to humanity than by making the wage system, in all its forms, an impossibility, and by rendering communism, which is the negation of wage-slavery, the only possible solution.

For even admitting that the collectivist modifica-
tion of the present system is possible, if introduced
gradually during a period of prosperity and peace –
though for my part I question its practicability even
under such conditions – it would become impossible
in a period of revolution, when the need of feeding
hungry millions would spring up with the first call
to arms. A political revolution can be accomplished
without shaking the foundations of industry, but
a revolution where the people lay hands upon
property will inevitably paralyse exchange and
production. The millions of public money flowing
into the Treasury would not suffice for paying wages
to the millions of out-of-works.

This point cannot be too much insisted upon; the
reorganization of industry on a new basis (and we
shall presently show how tremendous this problem
is) cannot be accomplished in a few days; nor, on the
other hand, will the people submit to be half starved
for years in order to oblige the theorists who uphold
the wage system. To tide over the period of stress
they will demand what they have always demanded
in such cases – communization of supplies – the
giving of rations.

It will be in vain to preach patience. The people
will be patient no longer, and if food is not forthcoming they will plunder the bakeries.

Then, if the people are not strong enough to carry all before them, they will be shot down, to give collectivism a fair field for experiment. To this end *'order'* must be maintained at any price – order, discipline, obedience! And as the capitalists will soon realize that when the people are shot down by those who call themselves revolutionists, the revolution itself will become hateful in the eyes of the masses, they will certainly lend their support to the champions of *order* – even though they are collectivists. In such a line of conduct, the capitalists will see a means of hereafter crushing the collectivists in their turn. And if 'order is established' in this fashion, the consequences are easy to foresee. Not content with shooting down the 'marauders', the faction of 'order' will search out the 'ringleaders of the mob'. They will set up again the law courts and reinstate the hangman. The most ardent revolutionists will be sent to the scaffold. It will be 1793 over again.

Do not let us forget how reaction triumphed in the last century. First the 'Hébertists' and 'the madmen' were guillotined – those whom Mignet, with the memory of the struggle fresh upon him, still called 'anarchists'. The Dantonists soon followed them; and when the party of Robespierre had guillotined these revolutionaries, they in their turn had to mount the scaffold; whereupon the people, sick of bloodshed, and seeing the Revolution lost, threw up the sponge, and let the reactionaries do their worst.

If 'order is restored', we say, the Social Democrats will hang the anarchists; the Fabians will hang the Social Democrats, and will in their turn be hanged by the reactionaries; and the revolution will come to an end.

But everything confirms us in the belief that the energy of the people will carry them far enough, and that, when the revolution takes place, the idea of anarchist communism will have gained ground. It is not an artificial idea. The people themselves have breathed it in our ear, and the number of communists is ever increasing, as the impossibility of any other solution becomes more and more evident.

And if the impetus of the people is strong enough, affairs will take a very different turn. Instead of plundering the bakers' shops one day, and starving the next, the people of the insurgent cities will take possession of the warehouses, the cattle markets – in fact of all the provision stores and of all the food to be had. The well-intentioned citizens, men and women both, will form themselves into bands of volunteers and address themselves to the task of making a rough general inventory of the contents of each shop and warehouse.

If such a revolution breaks out in France, namely,

in Paris, then in twenty-four hours the commune will know what Paris has not found out yet, in spite of its statistical committees, and what it never did find out during the siege of 1871 – the quantity of provisions it contains. In forty-eight hours millions of copies will be printed of the tables giving a sufficiently exact account of the available food, the places where it is stored, and the means of distribution.

In every block of houses, in every street, in every town ward, groups of volunteers will have been organized, and these commissariat volunteers will find it easy to work in unison and keep in touch with each other. If only the Jacobin bayonets do not get in the way; if only the self-styled 'scientific' theorists do not thrust themselves in to darken counsel! Or rather let them expound their muddle-headed theories as much as they like, provided they have no authority, no power! And that admirable spirit of organization inherent in the people, above all in every social grade of the French nation, but which they have so seldom been allowed to exercise, will initiate, even in so huge a city as Paris, and in the midst of a revolution, an immense guild of free workers, ready to furnish to each and all the necessary food.

Give the people a free hand, and in ten days the food service will be conducted with admirable regularity. Only those who have never seen the people hard at work, only those who have passed their lives buried among documents, can doubt it. Speak of the organizing genius of the 'Great Misunderstood', the people, to those who have seen it in Paris in the days of the barricades, or in London during the great dockers' strike, when half a million of starving folk had to be fed, and they will tell you how superior it is to the official ineptness of Bumbledom.

And even supposing we had to endure a certain amount of discomfort and confusion for a fortnight or a month, surely that would not matter very much. For the mass of the people it would still be an improvement on their former condition; and, besides, in times of revolution one can dine contentedly enough on a bit of bread and cheese while eagerly discussing events.

In any case, a system which springs up spontaneously, under stress of immediate need, will be infinitely preferable to anything invented between four walls by hidebound theorists sitting on any number of committees.

IV

The people of the great towns will be driven by force of circumstances to take possession of all the provisions, beginning with the barest necessaries, and gradually extending communism to other things, in order to satisfy the needs of all the citizens. The sooner it is done the better; the sooner it is done the less misery there will be and the less strife.

But upon what basis must society be organized in order that all may have their due share of food produce? This is the question that meets us at the outset.

We answer that there are no two ways of it. There is only one way in which communism can be established equitably, only one way which satisfies our instincts of justice and is at the same time practical; namely, the system already adopted by the agrarian communes of Europe.

Take for example a peasant commune, no matter where, even in France, where the Jacobins have done their best to destroy all communal usage. If the commune possesses woods and copses, then, so long as there is plenty of wood for all, everyone can take as much as he wants, without other let or hindrance than the public opinion of his neighbours. As to the timber-trees, which are always scarce, they have to be carefully apportioned.

The same with the communal pasture land; while there is enough and to spare, no limit is put to what the cattle of each homestead may consume, nor to the number of beasts grazing upon the pastures. Grazing grounds are not divided, nor is fodder doled out, unless there is scarcity. All the Swiss communes, and scores of thousands in France and Germany, wherever there is communal pasture land, practise this system.

And in the countries of Eastern Europe, where there are great forests and no scarcity of land, you find the peasants felling the trees as they need them, and cultivating as much of the soil as they require, without any thought of limiting each man's share of timber or of land. But the timber will be allowanced, and the land parcelled out, to each household according to its needs, as soon as either becomes scarce, as is already the case in Russia.

In a word, the system is this: no stint or limit to what the community possesses in abundance, but equal sharing and dividing of those commodities which are scarce or apt to run short. Of the 350 millions who inhabit Europe, 200 millions still follow this system of natural communism.

It is a fact worth remarking that the same system prevails in the great towns in the distribution of one commodity at least, which is found in abundance, the water supplied to each house.

As long as there is no fear of the supply running

short, no water company thinks of checking the consumption of water in each house. Take what you please! But during the great droughts, if there is any fear of the supply failing, the water companies know that all they have to do is to make known the fact, by means of a short advertisement in the papers, and the citizens will reduce their consumption of water and not let it run to waste.

But if water were actually scarce, what would be done? Recourse would be had to a system of rations. Such a measure is so natural, so inherent in common sense, that Paris twice asked to be put on rations during the two sieges which it underwent in 1871.

Is it necessary to go into details, to prepare tables, showing how the distribution of rations may work, to prove that it is just and equitable, infinitely more just and equitable than the existing state of things? All these tables and details will not serve to convince those of the middle classes, nor, alas, those of the workers tainted with middle-class prejudices, who regard the people as a mob of savages ready to fall upon and devour each other, as soon as the government ceases to direct affairs. But those only who have never seen the people resolve and act on their own initiative could doubt for a moment that if the masses were masters of the situation, they would distribute rations to each and all in strictest accordance with justice and equity.

If you were to give utterance, in any gathering of people, to the opinion that delicacies – game and such-like – should be reserved for the fastidious palates of aristocratic idlers, and black bread given to the sick in the hospitals, you would be hissed. But say at the same gathering, preach at the street corners and in the marketplaces, that the most tempting delicacies ought to be kept for the sick and feeble – especially for the sick. Say that if there are only five brace of partridge in the entire city, and only one case of sherry, they should go to sick people and convalescents. Say that after the sick come the children. For them the milk of the cows and goats should be reserved if there is not enough for all. To the children and the aged the last piece of meat, and to the strong man dry bread, if the community be reduced to that extremity.

Say, in a word, that if this or that article of consumption runs short, and has to be doled out, to those who have most need most should be given. Say that and see if you do not meet with universal agreement.

The man who is full-fed does not understand this, but the people do understand, and have always understood it; and even the child of luxury, if he is thrown on the street and comes into contact with the masses, even he will learn to understand.

The theorists – for whom the soldier's uniform and the barrack mess-table are civilization's last word – would like no doubt to start a regime of National Kitchens and 'Spartan Broth'. They would point out the advantages thereby gained, the economy in fuel and food, if such huge kitchens were established, where everyone could come for their rations of soup and bread and vegetables.

We do not question these advantages. We are well aware that important economies have already been achieved in this direction – as, for instance, when the handmill, or quern, and the baker's oven attached to each house were abandoned. We can see perfectly well that it would be more economical to cook broth for a hundred families at once, instead of lighting a hundred separate fires. We know, besides, that there are a thousand ways of preparing potatoes, but that cooked in one huge pot for a hundred families they would be just as good.

We know, in fact, that variety in cooking being a matter of the seasoning introduced by each cook or housewife, the cooking together of a hundredweight of potatoes would not prevent each cook or housewife from dressing and serving them in any way she pleased. And we know that stock made from meat can be converted into a hundred different soups to suit a hundred different tastes.

But though we are quite aware of all these facts, we still maintain that no one has a right to force the housewife to take her potatoes from the communal kitchen ready cooked if she prefers to cook them herself in her own pot on her own fire. And, above all, we should wish each one to be free to take his meals with his family, or with his friends, or even in a restaurant, if it seemed good to him.

Naturally, large public kitchens will spring up to take the place of the restaurants, where people are poisoned nowadays. Already the Parisian housewife gets the stock for her soup from the butcher, and transforms it into whatever soup she likes, and London housekeepers know that they can have a joint roasted, or an apple or rhubarb tart baked at the baker's for a trifling sum, thus economizing time and fuel. And when the communal kitchen – the common bakehouse of the future – is established, and people can get their food cooked without the risk of being cheated or poisoned, the custom will no doubt become general of going to the communal kitchen for the fundamental parts of the meal, leaving the last touches to be added as individual taste shall suggest.

But to make a hard and fast rule of this, to make

a duty of taking home our food ready cooked, that would be as repugnant to our modern minds as the ideas of the convent or the barrack – morbid ideas born in brains warped by tyranny or superstition.

'Who will have a right to the food of the commune?' will assuredly be the first question which we shall have to ask ourselves. Every township will answer for itself, and we are convinced that the answers will all be dictated by the sentiment of justice. Until labour is reorganized, as long as the disturbed period lasts, and while it is impossible to distinguish between inveterate idlers and genuine workers thrown out of work, the available food ought to be shared by all without exception. Those who have been enemies to the new order will hasten of their own accord to rid the commune of their presence. But it seems to us that the masses of the people, which have always been magnanimous, and have nothing of vindictiveness in their disposition, will be ready to share their bread with all who remain with them, conquered and conquerors alike. It will be no loss to the revolution to be inspired by such an idea, and, when work is set agoing again, the antagonists of yesterday will stand side by side in the same workshops. A society where work is free will have nothing to fear from idlers.

'But provisions will run short in a month!' our critics at once exclaim.

'So much the better,' say we. It will prove that for the first time on record the people have had enough to eat. As to the question of obtaining fresh supplies, we shall discuss the means in our next chapter.

V

By what means could a city in a state of revolution be supplied with food? We shall answer this question, but it is obvious that the means resorted to will depend on the character of the revolution in the provinces, and in neighbouring countries. If the entire nation, or, better still, if all Europe should accomplish the social revolution simultaneously, and start with thoroughgoing communism, our procedure would be simplified; but if only a few communities in Europe make the attempt, other means will have to be chosen. The circumstances will dictate the measures.

We are thus led, before we proceed further, to glance at the state of Europe, and, without pretending to prophesy, we may try to foresee what course the revolution will take, or at least what will be its essential features.

Certainly it would be very desirable that all

Europe should rise at once, that expropriation should be general, and that communistic principles should inspire all and sundry. Such a universal rising would do much to simplify the task of our century.

But all the signs lead us to believe that it will not take place. That the revolution will embrace Europe we do not doubt. If one of the four great continental capitals – Paris, Vienna, Brussels or Berlin – rises in revolution and overturns its government, it is almost certain that the three others will follow its example within a few weeks' time. It is, moreover, highly probable that the Peninsulas and even London and St Petersburg would not be long in following suit. But whether the revolution would everywhere exhibit the same characteristics is highly doubtful.

It is more than probable that expropriation will be everywhere carried into effect on a larger scale, and that this policy carried out by any one of the great nations of Europe will influence all the rest; yet the beginnings of the revolution will exhibit great local differences, and its course will vary in different countries. In 1789–93, the French peasantry took four years to finally rid themselves of the redemption of feudal rights, and the bourgeois to overthrow royalty. Let us keep that in mind, and therefore be prepared to see the revolution develop itself somewhat gradually. Let us not be disheartened if here and there its steps should move less rapidly. Whether it would take an avowedly socialist character in all European nations, at any rate at the beginning, is doubtful. Germany, be it remembered, is still realizing its dream of a united empire. Its advanced parties see visions of a Jacobin republic like that of 1848, and of the organization of labour according to Louis Blanc; while the French people, on the other hand, want above all things a free commune, whether it be a communist commune or not.

There is every reason to believe that, when the coming revolution takes place, Germany will go further than France went in 1793. The eighteenth-century Revolution in France was an advance on the English Revolution of the seventeenth, abolishing as it did at one stroke the power of the throne and the landed aristocracy, whose influence still survives in England. But, if Germany goes further and does greater things than France did in 1793, there can be no doubt that the ideas which will foster the birth of her revolution will be those of 1848; while the ideas which will inspire the revolution in Russia will probably be a combination of those of 1789 with those of 1848.

Without, however, attaching to these forecasts a greater importance than they merit, we may safely conclude this much: the revolution will take a different character in each of the different European nations; the point attained in the socialization of wealth will not be everywhere the same.

Will it therefore be necessary, as is sometimes suggested, that the nations in the vanguard of the movement should adapt their pace to those who lag behind? Must we wait till the communist revolution is ripe in all civilized countries? Clearly not! Even if it were a thing to be desired, it is not possible. History does not wait for the laggards.

Besides, we do not believe that in any one country the revolution will be accomplished at a stroke, in the twinkling of an eye, as some socialists dream.* It is highly probable that if one of the five or six large towns of France – Paris, Lyons, Marseilles, Lille,

---

* No fallacy more harmful has ever been spread than the fallacy of a 'one-day revolution', which is propagated in superficial socialist pamphlets speaking of the revolution of the 18th of March at Berlin, supposed (which is absolutely wrong) to have given Prussia its representative government. We saw well the harm made by such fallacies in Russia in 1905–7. The truth is that up to 1871 Prussia, like Russia of the present day, had a scrap of paper which could be described as a 'constitution', but it had no representative government. The Ministry imposed upon the nation, up till 1870, the budget it chose to propose.

Saint-Etienne, Bordeaux – were to proclaim the commune, the others would follow its example, and that many smaller towns would do the same. Probably also various mining districts and industrial centres would hasten to rid themselves of 'owners' and 'masters', and form themselves into free groups.

But many country places have not advanced to that point. Side by side with the revolutionized communes such places would remain in an expectant attitude, and would go on living on the individualist system. Undisturbed by visits of the bailiff or the tax-collector, the peasants would not be hostile to the revolutionaries, and thus, while profiting by the new state of affairs, they would defer the settlement of accounts with the local exploiters. But with that practical enthusiasm which always characterizes agrarian uprisings (witness the passionate toil of 1792) they would throw themselves into the task of cultivating the land, which, freed from taxes and mortgages, would become so much dearer to them.

As to other countries, revolution would break out everywhere, but revolution under divers aspects; in one country state socialism, in another federation; everywhere more or less socialism, not conforming to any particular rule.

VI

Let us now return to our city in revolt, and consider how its citizens can provide foodstuffs for themselves. How are the necessary provisions to be obtained if the nation as a whole has not accepted communism? This is the question to be solved. Take, for example, one of the large French towns – take the capital itself, for that matter. Paris consumes every year thousands of tons of grain, 400,000 head of oxen, 300,000 calves, 400,000 swine, and more than 2 million sheep, besides great quantities of game. This huge city devours, besides, more than 20 million pounds of butter, 200 million eggs, and other produce in like proportion.

It imports flour and grain from the United States and from Russia, Hungary, Italy, Egypt and the Indies; livestock from Germany, Italy, Spain – even Romania and Russia; and as for groceries, there is not a country in the world that it does not lay under contribution.

Now, let us see how Paris or any other great town could be revictualled by home-grown produce, supplies of which could be readily and willingly sent in from the provinces.

To those who put their trust in 'authority' the

question will appear quite simple. They would begin by establishing a strongly centralized government, furnished with all the machinery of coercion – the police, the army, the guillotine. This government would draw up a statement of all the produce contained in France. It would divide the country into districts of supply, and then *command* that a prescribed quantity of some particular foodstuff be sent to such a place on such a day, and delivered at such a station, to be there received on a given day by a specified official and stored in particular warehouses.

Now, we declare with the fullest conviction, not merely that such a solution is undesirable, but that it never could by any possibility be put into practice. It is wildly utopian!

Pen in hand, one may dream such a dream in the study, but in contact with reality it comes to nothing – this was proved in 1793; for, like all such theories, it leaves out of account the spirit of independence that is in man. The attempt would lead to a universal uprising, to three or four *Vendées*, to the villages rising against the towns, all the country up in arms defying the city for its arrogance in attempting to impose such a system upon the country.

We have already had too much of Jacobin utopias! Let us see if some other form of organization will meet the case.

During the great French Revolution, the provinces starved the large towns, and killed the Revolution. And yet it is a known fact that the production of grain in France during 1792–3 had not diminished; indeed, the evidence goes to show that it had increased. But after having taken possession of the manorial lands, after having reaped a harvest from them, the peasants would not part with their grain for paper-money. They withheld their produce, waiting for a rise in the price, or the introduction of gold. The most rigorous measures of the National Convention were without avail, and her executions failed to break up the ring, or force the farmers to sell their corn. For it is a matter of history that the commissaries of the Convention did not scruple to guillotine those who withheld their grain from the market, and pitilessly executed those who speculated in foodstuffs. All the same, the corn was not forthcoming, and the townsfolk suffered from famine.

But what was offered to the husbandman in exchange for this hard toil? Assignats, scraps of paper decreasing in value every day, promises of payment, which could not be kept. A £40 note would not purchase a pair of boots, and the peasant, very naturally, was not anxious to barter a year's toil for a piece of paper with which he could not even buy a shirt.

As long as worthless paper-money – whether called assignats or labour-notes – is offered to the peasant-producer it will always be the same. The country will withhold its produce, and the towns will suffer want, even if the recalcitrant peasants are guillotined as before.

We must offer to the peasant in exchange for his toil not worthless paper-money, but the manufactured articles of which he stands in immediate need. He lacks the proper implements to till the land, clothes to protect him properly from the inclemencies of the weather, lamps and oil to replace his miserable rushlight or tallow dip, spades, rakes, ploughs. All these things, under present conditions, the peasant is forced to do without, not because he does not feel the need of them, but because, in his life of struggle and privation, a thousand useful things are beyond his reach; because he has no money to buy them.

Let the town apply itself, without loss of time, to manufacturing all that the peasant needs, instead of fashioning gewgaws for the wives of rich citizens. Let the sewing machines of Paris be set to work on clothes for the country folk: workaday clothes and clothes for Sunday too, instead of costly evening dresses for the English and Russian landlords and the African gold-magnates' wives. Let the factories and foundries turn out agricultural implements, spades, rakes, and such-like, instead of waiting till the English send them to France, in exchange for French wines!

Let the towns send no more inspectors to the villages, wearing red, blue, or rainbow-coloured scarves, to convey to the peasant orders to take his produce to this place or that, but let them send friendly embassies to the country folk and bid them in brotherly fashion: 'Bring us your produce, and take from our stores and shops all the manufactured articles you please.' Then provisions would pour in on every side. The peasant would only withhold what he needed for his own use, and would send the rest into the cities, feeling *for the first time in the course of history* that these toiling townsfolk were his comrades – his brethren, and not his exploiters.

We shall be told, perhaps, that this would necessitate a complete transformation of industry. Well, yes, that is true of certain departments; but there are other branches which could be rapidly modified in such a way as to furnish the peasant with clothes, watches, furniture and the simple implements for which the towns make him pay such exorbitant prices at the present time. Weavers, tailors, shoemakers, tinsmiths, cabinet-makers and many other trades and crafts could easily direct their energies to the manufacture of useful and necessary articles, and abstain from producing mere luxuries. All that is needed is that the public mind should be thoroughly convinced of the necessity of this transformation, and should come to look upon it as an act of justice and of progress, and that it should no longer allow itself to be cheated by that dream, so dear to the theorists – the dream of a revolution which confines itself to taking possession of the profits of industry, and leaves production and commerce just as they are now.

This, then, is our view of the whole question. Cheat the peasant no longer with scraps of paper – be the sums inscribed upon them ever so large; but offer him in exchange for his produce the very *things* of which he, the tiller of the soil, stands in need. Then the fruits of the land will be poured into the towns. If this is not done there will be famine in our cities, and reaction and despair will follow in its train.

VII

All the great towns, we have said, buy their grain, their flour and their meat, not only from the provinces, but also from abroad. Foreign countries send Paris not only spices, fish and various dainties, but also immense quantities of corn and meat.

But when the revolution comes these cities will have to depend on foreign countries as little as possible. If Russian wheat, Italian or Indian rice, and Spanish or Hungarian wines abound in the markets of Western Europe, it is not that the countries which export them have a superabundance, or that such a produce grows there of itself, like the dandelion in the meadows. In Russia, for instance, the peasant works sixteen hours a day, and half starves from three to six months every year, in order to export the grain with which he pays the landlord and the state. Today the police appears in the Russian village as soon as the harvest is gathered in, and sells the peasant's last horse and last cow for arrears of taxes and rent due to the landlord, unless the victim immolates himself of his own accord by selling the grain to the exporters. Usually, rather than part with his livestock at a disadvantage, he keeps only a nine months' supply of grain, and sells the rest. Then, in order to sustain life until the next harvest, he mixes birch-bark and tares with his flour for three months, if it has been a good year, and for six if it has been bad, while in London they are eating biscuits made of his wheat.

But as soon as the revolution comes, the Russian peasant will keep bread enough for himself and his children; the Italian and Hungarian peasants will do the same; the Hindu, let us hope, will profit by these good examples; and the farmers of America will hardly be able to cover all the deficit in grain which Europe will experience. So it will not do to count on their contributions of wheat and maize satisfying all the wants.

Since all our middle-class civilization is based on the exploitation of inferior races and countries with less advanced industrial systems, the revolution will confer a boon at the very outset, by menacing that 'civilization', and allowing the so-called inferior races to free themselves.

But this great benefit will manifest itself by a steady and marked diminution of the food supplies pouring into the great cities of Western Europe.

It is difficult to predict the course of affairs in the provinces. On the one hand the slave of the soil will take advantage of the revolution to straighten his bowed back. Instead of working fourteen or fifteen hours a day, as he does at present, he will be at liberty to work only half that time, which of course would have the effect of decreasing the production of the principal articles of consumption – grain and meat.

But, on the other hand, there will be an increase of production as soon as the peasant realizes that he is no longer forced to support the idle rich by his toil.

New tracts of land will be cleared, new and improved machines set agoing.

'Never was the land so energetically cultivated as in 1792, when the peasant had taken back from the landlord the soil which he had coveted so long,' Michelet tells us, speaking of the Great Revolution.

Of course, before long, intensive culture would be within the reach of all. Improved machinery, chemical manures and all such matters would soon be supplied by the commune. But everything tends to indicate that at the outset there would be a falling off in agricultural products, in France and elsewhere.

In any case it would be wisest to count upon such a falling off of contributions from the provinces as well as from abroad. How is this falling off to be made good?

Why! By setting to work ourselves! No need to rack our brains for far-fetched panaceas when the remedy lies close at hand!

The large towns, as well as the villages, must undertake to till the soil. We must return to what biology calls 'the integration of functions' – after the division of labour, the taking up of it as a whole – this is the course followed throughout Nature.

Besides, philosophy apart, the force of circumstances would bring about this result. Let Paris see that at the end of eight months it will be running short of bread, and Paris will set to work to grow wheat.

Land will not be wanting, for it is round the great towns, and round Paris especially, that the parks and pleasure grounds of the landed gentry are to be found. These thousands of acres only await the skilled labour of the husbandman to surround Paris with fields infinitely more fertile and productive than the steppes of southern Russia, where the soil is dried up by the sun. Nor will labour be lacking. To what should the 2 million citizens of Paris turn their attention, when they would be no longer catering for the luxurious fads and amusements of Russian princes, Romanian grandees and wives of Berlin financiers?

With all the mechanical inventions of the century; with all the intelligence and technical skill of the worker accustomed to deal with complicated machinery; with inventors, chemists, professors of botany, practical botanists like the market-gardeners of Gennevilliers; with all the plant that they could use for multiplying and improving machinery; and, finally, with the organizing spirit of the Parisian people, their pluck and energy – with all these at its command, the agriculture of the anarchist commune of Paris would be a very different thing from the rude husbandry of the Ardennes.

Steam, electricity, the heat of the sun and the breath of the wind, will ere long be pressed into service. The steam plough and the steam harrow will quickly do the rough work of preparation, and the soil, thus cleaned and enriched, will only need the intelligent care of man, and of woman even more than man, to be clothed with luxuriant vegetation – not once but three or four times in the year.

Thus, learning the art of horticulture from experts, and trying experiments in different methods on small patches of soil reserved for the purpose, vying with each other to obtain the best returns, finding in physical exercise, without exhaustion or overwork, the health and strength which so often flags in cities – men, women and children will gladly turn to the labour of the fields, when it is no longer a slavish drudgery, but has become a pleasure, a festival, a renewal of health and joy.

'There are no barren lands; the earth is worth what man is worth' – that is the last word of modern agriculture. Ask of the earth, and she will give you bread, provided that you ask aright.

A district, though it were as small as the two departments of the Seine and the Seine-et-Oise, and with so great a city as Paris to feed, would be practically sufficient to grow upon it all the food supplies, which otherwise might fail to reach it.

The combination of agriculture and industry, the husbandman and the mechanic in the same individual – this is what anarchist communism will inevitably lead us to, if it starts fair with expropriation.

Let the revolution only get so far, and famine is not the enemy it will have to fear. No, the danger which will menace it lies in timidity, prejudice and half measures. The danger is where Danton saw it when he cried to France: 'De l'audace, de l'audace, et encore de l'audace.' The bold thought first, and the bold deed will not fail to follow.